EAAY TRANOE

WILLIS BARNSTONE, a professor of Spanish and Comparative Literature at Indiana University, is well-known for both his original poetry and his translations, particularly of Spanish and classical texts. His volume of poems *From This White Island* was nominated for a Pulitzer Prize in 1960. In 1961 he was a Guggenheim fellow in Spain where he wrote a critical study, *Antonio Machado: A Study of the Lyrical Speaker in the Poems*. Other publications include translations of *Eighty Poems of Antonio Machado; Sappho: Lyrics in the Original Greek;* and the medieval Latin bestiary, *Physiologus Theobaldi.*

Mr. Barnstone is editor of *Artes Hispanicas/ Hispanic Arts.*

GREEK LYRIC POETRY

GREEK LYRIC POETRY

Translated by
WILLIS BARNSTONE

Introduction by William E. McCulloh

Drawings by Helle Tzalos

INDIANA UNIVERSITY PRESS
Bloomington & London

TO
Helle Phaedra
who led me to Greece

and to my brother
Howard Barnstone

ACKNOWLEDGMENTS

Certain of these poems first appeared in the *Antioch Review, Arizona Quarterly, Chelsea Review, Chicago Review, Evergreen Review, Wesleyan Cardinal* and *The World's Love Poetry.*

Contents

Contents

THE BYZANTINE PERIOD

AUTHORS AND ANONYMOUS WORKS   OF
INDEFINITE PERIOD

GREEK LYRIC POETRY

Introduction

Suppose, in our time, the War actually comes. With no current refinements wasted, the elephantine blasts, fire storms, and fallout finish their appointed tasks. Several decades later the literary archaeologists from Tierra del Fuego and the Samoyedes rake loose from London's heaps part of a volume of literary criticism in which stand, entire, Yeats' lines "My fiftieth year had come and gone"— and the "Second Coming," with a few single lines quoted amid the unknown critic's comments. Then a gutted Pittsburgh mansion yields two charred anonymous sheets of a poem whose style—what can be seen of it—resembles Yeats. A fragmentary dictionary cites, as a rare alternate pronunciation of fanatic: "Fá-na-tic. Thus in W. B. Yeats' 'Remorse for Intemperate Speech.'" There are similar further recoveries, equally scanty. So much for the poet whom T. S. Eliot has called the greatest of the twentieth century.

But this has happened already, in time's glacial cataclysm, to the greatest lyric poet (so men say) of the West before the thirteenth century—to Sappho. And to Archilochos, whom some ancients paired with Homer. And to many others, the Herricks, Donnes, and Herberts of Greece's first lyric flowering. For however much one may take it as unmerited grace that one has at least Homer, at least the iceberg tip of the fifth century and its epigones, one must still question the providence which allowed from the vastly different age between—the Lyric Age of the seventh and sixth centuries[1]—only Pindar and the scraps for one other small book. That uniquely organic outgrowth of successive literary styles and forms in Greece—forms which are the ineluctable basis for most Western litera-

[1] Thus the title given it by A. R. Burn in *The Lyric Age of Greece* (London, 1960).

ture[2]—is thus desperately mutilated for us in what seems to have been its most explosively diverse and luxuriant phase.

Homer is the culmination of a long and now invisible tradition of heroic poetry which was the literary voice of a monarchical society. His heroes are the archetypal ancestors of the royalty in whose courts the epic lays flourished and whose values the bard celebrated. But, like Bach, he seems to have written in times which had already moved past his own poetic world. The city-state was beginning to displace the tribal monarchy. The conflict between monarchy and aristocracy had begun, and perhaps also that conflict between aristocracy and commons which led to the great tyrannies (somewhat like the dictatorships of our century) and—at least in some cities—to democracy. But most important for poetry, the poet had begun to emerge as an individual speaking for himself, not an impersonal celebrant of ancestral glory and doom.

While the elder Bach composed his *Art of Fugue "ad maiorem Dei gloriam,"* his sons were breaking the homophonic trail toward the secular divinity of the Beethoven symphony. And within the lifetime of "Homer" (though dates are of course uncertain), Archilochos, the first Western man whom we know as a personality, and the first European lyric poet of whom fragments remain, was fusing and transforming popular and anonymous song and dance into the personal poem. So it is with Archilochos that we must begin, the first historical Western personality, and for us, the impoverished heirs, the inceptor of European lyric.

The Forms of Greek Lyric

But here an academic detour is required. What we shall call Greek "lyric" poetry is in fact a cluster of several quite distinct types, each with its own tradition and development. "Lyric" means literally "accompanied by the lyre," and implies poetry that is sung, not spoken. Now it is

---

[2] See for example Gilbert Highet, *The Classical Tradition* (New York, 1957).

likely that all forms of Greek poetry originated in ritual performances which blended word, music, and dance. But in historical times only one branch of that poetry retained all three elements: the choral ode. *Choros,* for the Greeks, meant a performing group which both danced and sang. (Compare "choreography.") *Ôide* meant song. Chorodic poetry, then, remained closer to its ritual origins than did any of the other forms. It was associated with a variety of public ceremonies. Already in Homer one finds most of these mentioned or described.[3] There is the *Thrênos,* or dirge for the dead (the lament for Hektor, *Iliad* XXIV, 746ff.), which survives today as the requiem mass. There is the *Paian,* or hymn to Apollo (*Iliad* I, 472-4), of which some hymns of Hölderlin and Shelley are modern mutations. Of the *Hymenaios* or wedding song (*Iliad* XVIII, 493), Spenser's "Epithalamion," "O Promise Me," and the charivari are schizoid remnants. And compare the *Hyporchêma* or mimetic-narrative dance (*Odyssey* VIII, 261ff.) with *The Seven Deadly Sins* of Weil-Brecht-Balanchine. The *Prosôdion,* or processional song (still surviving in some religious services), is not found in Homer. Nor is the dithyramb, originally an intoxicated improvisation in honor of the god of ecstasy, Dionysos. According to Aristotle, though his claim is much disputed,[4] it was the dithyramb which took on dramatic form and became tragedy. If so, this is the most portentous of all chorodic forms: the bulk of European drama is its grandchild.

In the sixth-century choral odes came to be written in celebration of human, rather than divine, excellence. The *Enkômion* praised great men. Victors in the great athletic contests of Greece were honored in the *Epinîkion.* For those to whom the decathlon is not a revelation of one of the cardinal excellences of man, it seems curious that such should have been the occasion for the poetry of Pindar, who has been called "one of the four spiritual reasons for

[3] The classification given here is taken from C. M. Bowra's full discussion in the introduction to his *Greek Lyric Poetry* (Oxford, 1936. 2d ed., 1962).

[4] As, for example, in A. W. Pickard-Cambridge's *Dithyramb, Tragedy, and Comedy* (Oxford, 1927).

setting ourselves to the toil of mastering the Greek language."[5]

Throughout this apparent wilderness of chorodic types there are three nearly universal common features. First, the language is usually ornate and complex, with some features of the Doric dialect. Second, the typical choral ode (apart from drama) is composed of a series of paired and metrically identical stanzas, with each pair separated from the next by a stanza of similar but not identical metrical character. The pair consists of a strophe and antistrophe, or "turn" and "counter-turn." (These terms are thought to refer to the fact that the dance movements in the second stanza of each pair were exactly reversed from those of the first.) The third, dividing stanza is the epode. The metrical patterns in chorodic poetry are more complex than those of any other Greek poetry—in fact, more complex than any other European poetry except free verse. And the patterns of no two odes are identical. Diversity and regularity, freedom and balance, have never been more perfectly fused.

The third feature common to nearly all choral odes is the material of which the odes consist.[6] There are moral maxims. (In Pindar these can become abrupt revelations.) Individuals involved in the festival or celebration are mentioned. And—most important for literature—a myth is retold, often, as in Pindar, from a striking viewpoint, with daring ellipses and compressions in the narrative—the antipode to Homer's way. Alkman's *Partheneion*, the earliest choral ode to survive *in extenso*, exhibits all three of these elements.

There have been modern attempts at close imitation of the Greek choral ode. Among these are the choruses of Swinburne's *Erectheus* and Arnold's *Merope*, Gray's Pindaric odes, and some of the choruses in the Helena section of Goethe's *Faust II*.

With the elimination of the dancing chorus one reaches the second of the two forms of poetry which are, in the Greek sense, genuinely lyric: the solo song, or monody.

[5] Lewis Richard Farnell, *The Works of Pindar* (London, 1930), I, vii.
[6] Bowra, *Greek Lyric Poetry*, Introduction.

[4]

Monody is much closer to the usual modern lyric in its relative simplicity and its preoccupation with the poet's personal concerns. But ancient monody ranged more widely—into politics and satire, for example—than one would expect of "lyric" poetry. And unlike much modern lyric, the poem is never an utterly private communing of the poet with himself; it is always conceived of as addressed to an audience. The audience here, however, is usually not that of an official public occasion, but a private gathering—of disciples (Sappho), or of companions at a drinking party or *symposion* (Alkaios, Anakreon).

Monodies were composed of a single line or short stanza-pattern repeated throughout the poem. Unlike the choral lyric, the same stanza-pattern could be re-used in many poems, and the types of stanzas were limited. Two of the finest types are the Sapphic (employed by its eponym, for example, in the poems translated by Willis Barnstone under the titles "Prayer to Aphrodite" and "Seizure") and the Alcaeic (in which Alkaios's "Winter Evening" and "A Nation at Sea" were written[7]). Some idea of their character may perhaps be grasped in Tennyson's imitations:

Sapphic: Faded every violet, all the roses;
                Gone the promise glorious, and the victim,
                Broken in this anger of Aphrodite,
                     Yields to the victor.

Alcaeic: O mighty-mouthed inventor of harmonies,
                O skill'd to sing of Time and Eternity,
                     God-gifted organ voice of England,
                          Milton, a name to resound for ages.

Among modern imitations, one of Ezra Pound's earlier poems, "Apparuit," is in Sapphics, and a number of Swinburne's imitate monodic meters. But the one modern who consistently transcended imitation in his use of Greek monodic forms, who has earned a place with Horace for having snatched the lyric club from the Greek Hercules, is Hölderlin.

[7] All titles used in this introduction are those given by the translator. The originals are usually untitled.

In addition to poetry accompanied by music there are two further kinds of Greek verse which one today might roughly class as lyric. Both may originally have been sung, but early lost their music. Iambic poetry, allegedly the invention of Archilochos, was composed of lines predominantly in iambic or trochaic (the reverse of iambic) rhythms. It was at first chiefly employed, as one can see in Archilochos, Semonides of Amorgos, and Hipponax, for personal abuse, satire, and polemic. But even in Archilochos its range was wider (see for example the fragment "Moderation"). Solon used iambics to defend his political and economic policies at Athens.

The greatest offspring in Greek of iambic poetry was the dialog in Athenian drama. The drama is thus a hybrid of the chorodic and iambic traditions. But it has been further maintained that even Shakespeare's blank verse originally came, by way of Italian Renaissance imitations, from ancient drama and thus originally from the iambic poets.[8]

Finally, there is the elegiac poetry. Coleridge's adaptation of Schiller gives some idea of its basic unit, the elegiac couplet:

> In the hexameter rises the fountain's silvery column;
> In the pentameter aye falling in melody back.

The first line, the hexameter, has six feet of dactyls, often replaced in various feet by spondees (two long syllables). The second line, misnamed the "pentameter," is simply a hexameter with the second half of the third and sixth feet silent.

Of all forms of "lyric" verse, the elegiac has had the most nearly continuous existence, from the late eighth century or earlier into modern times. From the beginning it was used for highly diverse purposes.[9] 1) Like monody, it served to embellish the symposium. There it could speak of love and current political and military affairs, as it does in Kallinos, Mimnermos, and the collection attributed to

[8] Highet, *Classical Tradition*, p. 131.
[9] The categories here are approximately those of Bowra in his article "Elegiac Poetry, Greek," *Oxford Classical Dictionary* (Oxford, 1949).

Theognis. 2) It was used for long military and political harangues, such as those of Tyrtaios and Solon, and for historical narrative. 3) It was used in dedications inscribed on statues and other gifts to the gods. 4) It appeared on epitaphs, the short inscriptions on grave-markers. Simonides's epitaph for the Spartan dead at Thermopylae is the most famous (it was quoted in the 1960 Presidential campaign) of a noble company. 5) The form of the lament, especially in its later hybrid, the pastoral elegy, is the one best known in modern times. (Milton's "Lycidas" and *"Epitaphium Damonis,"* Gray's "Elegy," Shelley's "Adonais," Arnold's "Thyrsis.")

The elegiac form was transplanted into Latin and grew nobly in the Augustan period under the care of such men as Propertius and Ovid. It struggled bravely through the Middle Ages until the Renaissance gave it new life, and it survived into the nineteenth century for its finest harvest (apart from its mutation into the English heroic couplet) since the Augustans, in Goethe's *Roman Elegies,* and those of Hölderlin. Since then the couplet form itself has languished. But the spirit passed from Hölderlin into those poems supreme among all which bear the name elegy, the *Duino Elegies* of Rilke.

Development of Greek Lyric

So much for the forms of Greek lyric and their afterlife. It is time now to return to Archilochos and treat of the temporal phases of lyric. The subject is by nature erratic and fragmentary, and the following brash survey of the principal remains will suffer even more heavily from these defects. For full and proper treatment, the reader should consult the bibliography.

We have seen that the social changes in the late eighth century contributed to the development of the poem as individual expression. But much is owing to the innovating personality of Archilochos himself. Born a bastard, of a Greek father and a Thracian mother, he was an outsider from the start. His life as a free-lance soldier, moreover, intensified his alienation from group traditions. Thus thrown upon himself, he rejected the values of the aristocracy, particularly that supreme aristocratic value, Honor (which at the time was roughly chivalric in character). Honor, to the conventional aristocrat of his age, was something worth dying for, since death was in any case inevitable, and an "honorable" death gave one at least the secular immortality of renown. Says Sarpedon to Glaukos in the *Iliad* (XII, 322ff.), "Man, could we survive this war and live forever, deathless and strong, I would not be fighting out in front, nor would I urge you to this fray which gives us glory. But death in myriad forms is closing in—no mortal can slip past it. Come with me; no matter if another will boast over us, or we over him."

Archilochos, as his fragment "On His Shield" makes clear, chose another way. To throw away one's shield in a hasty retreat was not worse than death. It was simple common sense. What counted was not the deathless fame, but the tangible delights of the present, precious moment. Together with future glory Archilochos discarded the equally impalpable worth of present reputation; it was better to make enemies than to appease. Some would hold that the short fragment here titled "Proverb for a Great Scoundrel" refers in fact to the poet himself. If so, the image of the self-reliant, self-enclosed hedgehog is an apt one for this first on Europe's honorable roll of prickly, renegade poets.

Archilochos' revolution did not of course transform the whole of subsequent poetry. It seems to have been the regions of the Eastern Greeks, the Aiolians and Ionians of Asia Minor and the islands, which proved most receptive to the new spirit. Meanwhile at Sparta, the heart of the younger Western, or Dorian branch of Greek culture, Tyrtaios was composing martial elegies in which an older communal ethos still lived. The Spartans were the nearest approximation among the Greeks to the collectivist mentality. It is therefore fitting that their gift to the Lyric Age should have been the most collective of forms, the choral ode.

To be sure, as earlier mentioned, the choral ode had existed, in a sense, from the beginning of cult, and thus perhaps ever since the tribal organization of man. But the wealthy patronage of the Spartan state during its years of peaceful abundance, in the later seventh century, attracted talented poets and gave them the means to produce their choruses for the public festivals. Significantly, most of the earlier of these commissioned poets were from the East, the older and subtler culture. The Eastern influence and the years of peace are perhaps the explanation for the un-Spartan playfulness and charm of the first surviving choral poet, Alkman.

Even in the choral form—a clear mark of the Lyric Age —one hears the voice of Alkman the individual. One of the most impressive aspects of that voice is its vivid perception of nature. Alkman was apparently the first to distinguish four seasons (rather than three). And, as in the poem "Rest," he shows a sense for the life of the inanimate world. "Rest" has suggested to some a parallel with Goethe's "Über allen Gipfeln." But it has further links with Rilke and Jeffers.

Until Simonides, choral poetry after Alkman is attested only in a bitterly small collection of scraps. Stesichoros, a native Dorian (this time from the far West, from Sicily), is credited with the introduction of greatly extended mythical narratives into the choral ode. The loss of his *Oresteia* or *Helen* was perhaps as irreparable as we should judge the perishing of Keats's "Eve of St. Agnes." Ibykos (he too from the far West) has at least left us with enough to establish that we have certainly lost much fine poetry.

With Ibykos we must touch on a matter which needs less belaboring today than it might have in the past. Much of Greek love poetry is about homosexual love. Greek society in general, and particularly in Dorian lands, was so arranged that women could not readily become full emotional companions of men. Marriage was often a purely practical affair entered upon by a man in his middle thirties for the purpose of raising a family. The wife was essentially a housekeeper. Consequently the deepest erotic experiences were frequently—and for the poetry of the Lyric Age, predominantly—homosexual, between older and younger men, and between older and younger women. Often, of course, the affairs were mere adventures in the

[9]

flesh. At other times they were as luminous and mature as any of the heterosexual passions of later ages. In our century Kavafis and George have shown in their poetry, as nearly as is possible in a different society, what pederasty could mean to the Greeks.

Ibykos brings choral poetry down to somewhere in the middle of the sixth century B.C. We must return to the end of the seventh for the commencement and, at the same time, the climax of monody.

Here Eastern Greece (Asia Minor and the islands)—the Aiolic island of Lesbos in particular—is the focus of creation. Alkaios and Sappho, both aristocrats of Lesbos, were contemporaries, and both in their own way reveal at its most intense the subjective individualism of Archilochos, now winged with lyric meters and those melodies which for us must be unheard.

The times were bad for aristocrats—both Alkaios and Sappho were exiled by a middle-class tyranny—and much of Alkaios' poetry is that of a militant reactionary. Other poems, archetypes of their kind, are devoted to the delights of the drinking party, whether as refuge from the outer political darkness or as a brief forgetting of the darkness of death.

In the poems of Sappho hardly a whiff of politics appears. Her persistent subjects are family, private friends and foes, and love. One view holds that she was head of a cult which was at the same time a finishing school for girls of the aristocracy—a cult devoted to poetry and Aphrodite—no mere symbol of beauty and love, but the genuine goddess. From within the group of her pupils she may have found her favorites. With these perhaps she shared that epiphany of her goddess of which she sings in her only wholly surviving poem, "Prayer to Aphrodite."

Simplicity and directness are the manner of all monody, in contrast to choral poetry. In Sappho these qualities are at their highest. For many, therefore, Sappho in her precious rags will stand above Pindar in his full effulgent robes at the thin-aired pinnacle of ancient lyric.

More than a full generation after Sappho comes the next and last personality in ancient monody. Anakreon, again from the East, but this time Ionia, became in popular legend a sort of poetic Silenus: a lovable, drunken, old infatuate. But, somewhat incongruously, this Silenus displays a deft, ironic wit which later imitators (the many anonymous authors of the *Anakreonteia*), playful and delightful as they often are, could not fully reproduce. It is, from our retrospective vantage, hard to believe that readers for centuries could have accepted the *Anakreonteia* as Anakreon's own.

The monodic strand in the Lyric Age comes to an end in a series of anonymous *Skolia* or drinking songs. These *Skolia* are the only native Athenian contribution, apart from Solon, to the poetry of the Lyric Age. Some of them are quite strong and vivid, but one could not guess from them that the fifth century in literature was to belong to Athens.

Three figures close the great period of Greek lyric. All three were choral poets chiefly, and were closely associated through family ties or rivalry. Simonides was uncle of Bakchylides. Pindar strove, sometimes bitterly, with both.

Simonides, eldest of the three, seems in many ways more modern, more a man of the fifth century, than the other two. Such things as his poem in criticism of Kleoboulos and his lecture-poem to Skopas on the limits of mortal virtue reflect a critical, intellectualist strain in Simonides, a readiness to modify received standards not, as with Archilochos, by mere subjective vehemence, but by rational judgment. His short fragment on "Arete" (virtue or excellence) is one of several poems which show a tendency toward dealing with abstract entities rather than traditional mythological divinities.

Like Pindar and Bakchylides, Simonides frequented the mansions of the great where his skills were welcomed and rewarded. But he seems to have given his ultimate sympathies to Athenian democracy, the fifth century's wave of the future. In his style he was celebrated for the controlled, vivid sobriety which can be seen in the long fragment on Danaë and Perseus.

Bakchylides survived in an even more fragmentary state than his uncle until 1896, when Egyptian sands surren-

dered a papyrus containing a tolerable proportion of his
works. The odes of Bakchylides, as we can now see, are
fluent, attractive, and often of great power.

Pindar, who deserves—even in translation—a volume of
his own (and has received it in Richmond Lattimore's fine
versions), must here be dealt with even more inadequately
than all who have gone before. Unlike Simonides, he was
not at home in the new currents of the fifth century. Like
Homer and Bach, he is the culmination of a tradition—the
chorodic—which the times were leaving behind. He was
most in his element not at democratic Athens, but in
Aigina and Thebes (the chief city of his native Boiotia)—
the cultural dinosaurs of the age. Proud, aloof, assured of
his genius, and wonderstruck by the brief, god-sent radiance of mortal excellence, he is deservedly the "Theban
eagle." For some of those who cleave the knotted oak and
swirling ocean of his Greek, there is no greater lyric in the
world.

After Pindar there is much that is brilliant, touching,
and entertaining in the lyric forms, but the highest ener-
gies in Greek literature are now found in drama, history,
oratory, and philosophy. There were of course still prac-
titioners of chorody and monody; even Aristotle tried his
hand at the former and wrought yeomanly. But a new
musical style increasingly subdued the text to mere li-
bretto. The predominant form for pure poetry was hence-
forth the elegiac epigram.

Elegiac poetry and iambic poetry after Archilochos have
been left to one side in our review thus far. Most of the
significant poets in both *genres* have been mentioned
above in the initial discussion of the forms of Greek lyric.
It should be noted that a fraction of the poetry of Archilochos and Anakreon is in elegiacs, and that a few iambic
lines of Anakreon survive. The elegiac epigrams of Simonides are, next to the work of Theognis, the largest body of
elegiac poetry by one man to survive before the third
century. Judging from the remains, the epigram, apart
from anonymous inscriptions, did not greatly flourish in
the latter part of the fifth and in the fourth centuries. The
epigrams some think to be Plato's, if in fact they do

belong to this period, are the one bright patch in these years.

But in the third century, at the hands of Asklepiades, Kallimachos, and their successors, epigram acquired new range and freshness. The short, pointed poem, usually in elegiacs—whether erotic, epitaph (real or simulated), satirical, or gnomic—became a popular lyric form.

And so it remained for all the succeeding centuries of Greek as an ancient language. Scholars and litterateurs, while Rome was refocusing the world, continued to refine a form which had lost touch with any vital, transforming, outside forces. But frozen as it was, the epigram could still gleam, most brightly in such men as Meleagros, Philodemos, Marcus Argentarius, grim Palladas—and even in the sixth-century A.D. Byzantine, Paulus Silentiarius. Gathered four times or more in successive collections, the harvest of epigram which is the *Greek Anthology* was stored in roughly its present form by Constantine Cephalas in the tenth century.

The death which came thus slowly to the Greek lyric can come to no other poetry with such apt grace. For in no other poetry does the conviction of the bitter, lesser glory of mortal works dwell so near the center. (The Roman poet mars his work by hollow boasts of immortality; the later West has Christianity flowing ambiguously in its heart.)

Greek lyric lives, of course, in another way—as part of the enriching stream from which each new age of poetry draws. "Death by Water" in *The Waste Land* is a form taken from the *Anthology*. Pound writes poems after Ibykos and Sappho. Salvatore Quasimodo translates the Greek lyricists. And those researchers of atomic rubble, with whom we began, could find a fit Hellenic epitaph for all our troublesome days in Yeats' lines for his own tomb:

> Cast a cold eye
> On life, on death.
> Horseman, pass by!

William E. McCulloh

A Note on Selections, Texts and Translation

Fire, religion and time have treated the lyric poetry of ancient Greece very poorly. Texts have disappeared by intention and through neglect. Today there is little hope of finding original papyrus manuscripts in Greece, for papyrus cannot easily survive in even the relatively dry climate of Greece.[1] Only in waterless parts of Egypt, in the rubbish heaps of antiquity, may ancient documents still be preserved, buried in tombs or with ancient cities under the sand. Indeed, there is always hope that the sands of some provincial city of Egypt will yield a new poem or fragment, such as the odes and dithyrambs of Bakchylides or Alkman's choral ode found in 1896 at Oxyrhynchos.

In what has survived—a small percent of the important lyric poetry—we still have enough to comprise one of man's great achievements in the arts. For we have poems by Sappho, Pindar, Bakchylides, Meleagros, Archilochos, Simonides, Alkaios, Anakreon and many others. The largest single collections are the victory odes of Pindar and the more than four thousand poems in the *Greek* or *Palatine Anthology*. A very large proportion of Greek lyric poetry survives as exempla quoted in studies of Greek and Latin scholars.

A single line in Greek by Sappho or an elegiac couplet ascribed to Plato may be precious to us in its own right:

WORLD

I could not hope
to touch the sky
with my two arms.   (Sappho)

---

[1] In 1961, for the first time, original papyrus was found in continental Greece, at Dervani (Lagada). See Herbert Hunger, "Papyrusfund in Griechenland," *Chronique d'Égypte*, tome xxxvii, no. 74, July, 1962.

or

> I am a sailor's tomb. Beside me lies a farmer.
> Hell is the same, under the land and sea.   (Plato)

But lines from Greek lyric poetry may also be precious when they are all we have left from which to form an image of an ancient poet. Because, therefore, the number of poems from shorter lyric poetry is so limited, I have translated virtually all the true lyric poems and intelligible fragments—monodic and choral—from the poets of the sixth and seventh centuries B.C, with the exception of Pindar and Bakchylides, who are represented only in part. By considering fragments and epigrams one may perhaps read enough lines from poets like Archilochos, Anakreon, Alkaios, Ibykos, Alkman, to see them in at least clear profile. Of the later poets, found in the *Greek* or *Palatine Anthology*, I have tried to make a generous selection of the better poems.

But the very fact that ancient papyri and later copies of Greek lyrics have been so maltreated makes one all the more mindful of omissions, and these too should be stated. From Pindar I have translated only a selection of the odes and fragments. Pindar's victory odes, a book in themselves, may be read in the luminous translations in Richmond Lattimore's *The Odes of Pindar*. There is also the serious omission of some longer elegiac and iambic poems. Thus while Tyrtaios, Semonides, Solon and Xenophanes are well represented, they have been denied inclusion of one or more of their significant extant compositions.[2] It is a tangible omission, however, which a later edition may hopefully correct. Another edition might also include a larger selection of sepulchral inscriptions.

---

[2] In this anthology the *lyric* poem is emphasized. For this reason excerpts are not given from epic poetry or from the plays. In using the word *lyric* no rigid definition is intended, e.g., the early Greek concept of lyric poems for the lyre as opposed to elegiac poems for the flute. Rather, lyric here simply means a short poem that sings. In this sense, and this alone, I have given preference to the more purely lyrical pieces from the Greek poets. The longer poems in elegiac couplets tend at times, like heroic couplets in English, to become essays in verse. This is true of longer poems of Tyrtaios, Semonides, Solon and Xenophanes.

More painful is the omission of many longer poems by Bakchylides. While he is represented here, the entire opus —thirteen epinikia, six dithyrambs and various short pieces—appears in lively translation in Robert Fagles' recent book, *Bacchylides: Complete Poems*, which both fills the gap and conveys the narrative eloquence and pristine imagery of this neglected poet. Bakchylides, like Thomas Traherne, is a relatively recent discovery; though there is as yet no piggyback tradition of praise—indeed, he has not been considered on his own but has been consistently and foolishly downgraded as a secondary Pindar—he is assured of his ancient place in the canon of the nine lyric poets.

The most formidable problem in translating from Greek has been to find a just approximation of Greek stanza forms and meter. It is at least consoling that there can never be a single solution for the transfer of prosodic techniques from one language to another. Poems in ancient Greek were composed primarily to be sung, chanted or recited, to be heard not read. In the original papyrus scripts the words were all run together as in Sanscrit. There were no indentations of shorter lines as in later manuscripts, for the poetic lines were also run together. Only capital letters were used. Thus even the question of whether English lines should begin with upper- or lower-case letters has no real precedence in the original scripts, and the most faithful translations would use upper-case letters exclusively. So, the first stanza of Sappho's poem to Anaktoria might read,

SOMESAYCAVALRYANDOTHERSCLAIM
INFANTRYORAFLEETOFLONGOARSIS
THESUPREMESIGHTONTHEBLACKEAR
TH.ISAYITIS

Even the stanzaic appearance of a Sapphic hymn or a Simonidean epigram as printed traditionally in Greek texts was determined by later scholars on the basis of metrical pauses.

I have tried to give order to these translations in several ways. To approximate the easy conversational flow of

many of the Greek poems, I have more often given a
syllabic rather than an accentual regularity to the lines.
An exception is the longer elegiac poem where the force-
ful dactyls seemed to call for a regular (though free-fall-
ing) beat in alternating lines of equal feet. In the matter
of diction, it is important to remember that the Greeks,
as most poets in the past—a Spenser or Kavafis excepted
—wrote in a language which seemed natural and contemporary to their readers.[3] My intention has been to use a
contemporary idiom, generally chaste, but colloquial as
the occasion suggests.

Until very recently, it has been a uniform practice to
impose rhyme on poems translated from ancient Greek.
But the Greeks did not use end rhyme as a common poetic
device. Rhyme was used only in rare instances, usually
for humor or satire (see Palladas, 550), and so rhyme is
not used in these translations. In most of the poems I
have tried to retain the stanzaic patterns suggested by the
metrical stops in the Greek texts. In others I have been
more original, or perhaps perverse, in seeking an equivalent of the Greek. I am especially guilty of license where
I seek to convey the humor of *Greek Anthology* epigrams.

In most cases the Greek rather than Latinized spelling
has been followed, thus Alkaios and Theokritos, not Alcaeus and Theocritus. In recent years the English trans-
literation of Greek words has become common and it is,
I believe, essentially more pleasant and satisfying to read.
It is a new practice, however, with rules unfixed, used
differently by different hands; I am aware of instances
where I have not been entirely consistent where the sin
of inconsistency is in the end less gauche than the virtue
of absolute order. So, while making the reader aware that
Pindar and Plato are really Pindaros and Platon, I have
persisted in referring to them as Plato and Pindar. Perhaps in a few years when original places and texts are
more familiar to us than English maps and translations,
we shall speak of Livorno, not Leghorn, Thessalonike not
Salonika, and even Pindaros not Pindar.

[3] Many writers did use archaic Homeric words and phrases, but this too
was at least natural in common poetic usage.

I have used standard recent texts: Lobel and Page, Diehl, Bowra (Pindar), Gow (Theokritos) and Loeb Library editions. I have also gone to Italian, French and modern Greek editions where they have been helpful. For some of the earlier poets, especially Sappho, I have in some cases followed the conjectural reconstructions of Treu (*Sappho Lieder*), Edmonds (Loeb Library) and Page (*Sappho and Alcaeus*)—when the only alternative to the reconstructed text is no poem at all. But I have misgivings about this. However, where a mutilated text can be used, it often offers, quite accidentally, very striking effects; in such poems as Sappho's "Age and Light," "Dream" and "The Laurel Tree," the very poverty of the lacuna-ridden text contributes a poignancy and quality of modernity which the reconstructed text lacks.

In innumerable cases there are variant readings in the Greek texts. I have usually followed the more recent editions.

A word about titles. All the poems included here have titles, yet few of these are traditional in the Greek. Why use titles then in English translations? Most of the poems and fragments are quotations found in other ancient writings. Though sometimes merely grammatical in nature, the context in which the poem appears usually gives additional information about the complete poem. The titles here are primarily informational, based on contextual information or on common ancient allusions with which a modern reader may be unfamiliar. Hopefully, titles will serve to replace lengthy footnotes and make the poems more complete.

Ideally, poetry in translation should one day lead a reader to a reading of the poem in the original tongue. The poem in its native phonemes, we often forget, was primarily a poem, and a good one, presumably, if chosen for translation. A poem in translation should be faithful, if to anything, to this primary quality of the original— that of its being an effective poem.

With this in mind we may say something about the general possibilities of poetry in translation. Many banal ideas are commonly held about the disadvantages of

poetry in translation—this despite the modern additions
to our language of verse translations by Lattimore, Fitts,
Fitzgerald, Wilbur, Lowell or Auden. Poems may be
poorly translated, as they may have been poorly written
originally, but they are not necessarily poorer or better
than the original—though the translator must secretly and
vainly aim for the latter. The quality of the poem in
translation will depend on the translator's skill in writing
poetry in his own language in the act of translating. If he
is T. S. Eliot translating Saint-Jean Perse or Mallarmé
translating Poe or the scholars of the King James Version
translating the psalms, the result may indeed be superior
—or at the very least equal. Only one thing is certain:
the poem in translation will be different. The translator's
task, then, is to produce a faithful forgery. The quality
and resemblance of the new product to the old lie somewhere between such fidelity and fraud.

But it is said that certain memorable lines or phrases
cannot be expressed in any other language. Yet it should
also be said that while at times we must lose, at others
we gain, and the good translator will take advantage of
the text, improving upon the weaker lines of the original,
while doing his best with the best. More important, it is
forgotten that translation provides an opportunity for
languages to interact upon each other, for one tongue to
alter and enrich the possibilities of expression in another.
In the past some translated works have changed both
literary language and tradition: notably the Petrarchan
sonnet, Luther's Bible, Judith Gautier's haiku. Milton went
as naturally to the King James Version for vocabulary as
Shakespeare turned to Holinshed for plots; when Rim-
baud's *Illuminations* were translated into English, the tradition of our literature was expanded to the extent that
diction and subject never before found in English were
presented to us.

In a word, the quality of a work in translation is de-
pendent on the translator's skills. His forgery is not necessarily better or worse than the original or than other
works in his own language; it is only necessarily different

—and here the difference, if new and striking, may extend the verbal and thematic borders of his own literature. And as a corollary to his work the new poem may also be seen as an essay into literary criticism, a reading, a creative *explication de texte.*

Discussion of translations of poetry usually confuses *kind* with *value.* One type of translation is thought to be intrinsically superior to others, be it free translation, close translation, poetry *after,* imitation, metaphrase, paraphrase, etc. In the critic's mind the quality of a translation often depends on how closely it conforms to his own preferred method. This error of descriptive rather than evaluative criticism—where kind determines value—probably occurs more often in regard to poetry translation than in any other form of literary criticism. But in the end, method is secondary, and determines neither the virtues nor sins of a poem. The translator need only clearly and honestly indicate his method—whatever it is—and then be judged, not on this choice, but on the quality of the new poem. If the new poem is good, the translator as artist will be performing his ancient function of retelling in his own form, a given content he has overheard from the immediate or the distant past.

I wish to thank William McCulloh for preparing the headnotes and Patricia Johnson for aid in preparing the glossary and index. I also wish to acknowledge my warm gratitude to Donald Reis, friend and editor for many years, and to my dear friends, John Dessauer, Walter and Edith Albee, John Vint, and Bernard Perry, for their help and their confidence.

Willis Barnstone

[21]

The Greek Period

Archilochos

According to the most probable view, Archilochos lived during the latter half of the eighth century B.C. *(The event referred to in "An Eclipse of the Sun" may have occurred either in 711* B.C. *or 647* B.C.*) He was the son of Telesikles, a nobleman of the island of Paros, and a slave-woman: hence, a bastard. He took part in the Parian colonization of the island of Thasos and seems to have spent most of his life as a soldier in the pay of his country. The only striking event in his life which has been preserved in the tradition is the "Lykambes affair." Lykambes, a nobleman, promised his daughter Neoboule to Archilochos and then went back on the promise. Archilochos took revenge in the poetic invective which has ever since been regarded (too narrowly) as his special gift. The legend that the potency of his satire produced the suicide of Neoboule, or Lykambes, or the whole family, is probably only legend. In later years, according to some interpreters of the fragments, Neoboule became a prostitute and even made advances to Archilochos, who rejected her with bitter comments on his former love. Archilochos died in battle. A cult in his honor was later established on Paros, and, by the third century* B.C., *his shrine had become a center for scholars.*

Chief works: 1) elegies dealing with warfare, consolation ("On Friends Lost at Sea"), personal expression, conviviality; 2) epodes (stanzas composed of several distinct meters) of personal or satirical content, often employing illustrative narratives— especially fable ("An Animal Appeals to Zeus"); 3) poems in iambic or trochaic meters, of satirical, personal, hortatory or narrative content. (The trochaic tetrameter was the popular equivalent of the more aristocratic narrative meter, the dactylic hexameter.)

Archilochos' language is chiefly the Ionic of his day, but in the elegies it is strongly influenced by Homeric diction.

As suggested in the Introduction, the ambiguous

[25]

*social position of Archilochos probably helped to
make him the spokesman par excellence of the new
spirit of the Lyric Age. This spirit included a
preoccupation with the "now," "here," and "I" (as
Adrados has said*), rather than with an archetypical
past. It further manifested a greatly increased sense
for man's helpless subjection to circumstance
("Providence," "Moderation").*

*Archilochos exercised considerable influence in
various ways over Kallimachos (iambics), Catullus
(satire), and Horace (epode).*

The iambus was invented by
Archilochos of Paros.
CLEMENT OF ALEXANDRIA, Miscellanies†

Of the three iambic writers in Aristarchos' canon,
the one who achieves the greatest mastery is
Archilochos. We find in him the most developed
sense of expression, with terse and vigorous
phrasing, and abundance of blood and muscle.
QUINTILIAN, Guide to Oratory

I would shun the poisonous tooth of slander.
Though removed in time, I have seen the
cantankerous Archilochos in poverty because he
fattened on the abuse of enemies.
PINDAR, Pythian Ode 2

In this grave lies Archilochos whom the Muses
guided to the writing of furious iambics to preserve
the supremacy of Homer's dactyls.
ADRIANOS, Palatine Anthology

---

* Francisco R. Adrados, *Líricos griegos: elegiacos y yambógraphos arcaicos* (Barcelona, 1956), I, 15.
† Clement is in error here.

1   THASOS AND SICILY

                    This wheatless island
stands like a donkey's back. It bristles
with a tangle of wild woodland.
                    Oh,
there is no country so beautiful,
no sensual earth that keys my passion
as these plains around the river Siris.*

2   AN ISLAND IN THE NORTH AIGAIAN
All, O all the calamities of all the Hellenes
are set loose on this battleground in Thasos.

3   THE DOUBLECROSS†
Let brawling waves beat his ship
against the shore, and have the mop-haired
    Thracians
take him naked at Salmydessos,
and he will suffer a thousand calamities
as he chews the bread of slaves.
His body will stiffen in freezing surf
as he wrestles with slimy seaweed,
and his teeth will rattle like a helpless dog,
flopped on his belly in the surge,
puking out the brine. Let me watch him grovel
in mud—for the wrong he did me:
as a traitor he trampled on our good faith,
he who was once my comrade.

4   PAROS FIGS
Say goodbye to the island Paros,
farewell to its figs and the seafaring life.

* These two separate fragments are found together.
† This poem is also ascribed to Hipponax.

5 THREAT

Let the stone of Tantalos
no longer overhang this island.

6 WAR

Look, Glaukos, how heavy seawaves leap skyward!
Over the Gyrai rocks
hangs a black cloud, a signal of winter storm.

From the unforeseen comes fear.

7 A VESSEL OF WINE

Go take your cup and walk along the timber deck
of our roaming ship; drain the hollow casks
of all their red wine. How can we stay sober
on the watch when all the rest are drunk?

8 A DROWNING

They laid down their lives
in the arms of waves.

9 SHIPWRECK

The vessel wavered on the cutting edge
between the stormwinds and the waves.

10 PRAYER AT SEA

Often, when their vessel was threatened by the
gray salty sea,
they prayed to Athene of the lovely braids for
sweet return.

11 ON FRIENDS LOST AT SEA

If you irritate the wound, Perikles, no man
in our city will enjoy the festivities.
These men were washed under by the thudding
seawaves,

and the hearts in our chest are swollen with pain.
Yet against this incurable misery, the gods
give us the harsh medicine of endurance.
Sorrows come and go, friend, and now they strike
    us
and we look with horror on the bleeding sores,
yet tomorrow others will mourn the dead. I tell you,
hold back your feminine tears and endure.

12   ON THE LACK OF PROPER BURNING
      AND BURIAL FOR HIS BROTHER-IN-LAW
      WHO WAS SHIPWRECKED

If only his head and handsome limbs
had been wrapped in white burial cloth
and touched by Hephaistos' hand of fire.

13   AN ECLIPSE OF THE SUN

Nothing in the world can surprise me now. Nothing
is impossible or too wonderful, for Zeus, father
of the Olympians, has turned midday into black
    night
by shielding light from the blossoming sun,
and now dark terror hangs over mankind.
    Anything
may happen, so do not be amazed if beasts
on dry land seek pasture with dolphins in
the ocean, and those beasts who loved sunny hills
love crashing seawaves more than the warm
    mainland.

14   DAWN

Dawn was rising full white.

15   GIRL

A spray of myrtle and beauty of a rose
were happiness in her hands, and her hair
fell as darkness on her back and shoulders.

[29]

16   ON PASIPHILE, A FRIEND OF ALL
As the figtree on its rock feeds many crows,
    so this simple girl sleeps with strangers.

17   SUDDEN LOVE
And to fall upon her heaving belly,
and thrust your groin into her groin,
your thighs between her thighs.

18   ON THE MALE ORGAN
Feeble now are the muscles in my mushroom.

19   LIKE A DONKEY
His penis is swollen
like a donkey from Priene
taking his fill of barley.

20   QUALITIES OF A GIRLFRIEND
She is a common woman for rent,
but what sensuality and fat ankles.
O fat whore for hire!

21   RICHES
Enormous was the gold he amassed
from many years of work,
but all
fell into the luscious arms
of a common whore.

22   PROVIDENCE
Let the gods take care of everything. Many times
they resurrect a man whom disaster left lying
face down on the black earth. Many times they
    topple

a man and pin him, back to the soil, though he
was solid on his feet. A multitude of evils
batters him as he wanders hungry and mad.

23 ON DEAD ANIMALS
Many of them, I hope, will be dried up
by the sharp rays of the sun in its zenith,
by the sun in the time of the Dog Star.

24 PROVERB FOR A GREAT SCOUNDREL
The fox knows many tricks,
the hedgehog only one. A good one.

25 HIS TWO VIRTUES
I am a servant of the kingly wargod Enyalios
and am also skilled in the lovely arts.

26 WINE OF NAXOS IS LIKE NECTAR
BUT HIS JAVELIN IS MUCH MORE
My javelin is good white bread and Ismarian wine.
When I find rest on my javelin I drink wine.

27 ON THE SHORT-HAIRED WARRIORS IN THE
LELANTINE WAR BETWEEN CHALKIS AND
ERETRIA WHO AGREED NOT TO USE MISSILE
WEAPONS
Perhaps fewer bows will be stretched and slings
hurled
when Ares begins battle on the noisy plain,
but then the mournful labor of the sword is worse.

This is warfare in which the spear-famed islanders
from Euboia are godlike and easily masterful.

28 APHRODITE IS CENSURED

Passionate love relentlessly twists a cord
under my heart and spreads deep mist on my eyes,
stealing the unguarded brains from my head.

29 ON HIS SHIELD

Well, what if some barbaric Thracian glories
in the perfect shield I left under a bush?
I was sorry to leave it—but I saved my skin.
Does it matter? O hell, I'll buy a better one.

30 MY KIND OF GENERAL

I don't like a general
who towers over the troops,
lordly with elegant locks
and trim mustachios.
Give me a stumpy soldier
glaringly bowlegged,
yet rockfirm on his feet,
and in his heart a giant.

31 CHARON THE CARPENTER

The gold booty of Gyges means nothing to me.
I don't envy that Lydian king, nor am I jealous
of what gods can do, nor of the tyrants' great
powers. All these are realms beyond my vision.

32 MERCENARY FRIENDSHIP

Glaukos, soldier of fortune, will be your friend
until he begins to fight.

33 WEDDING DEDICATION

When Alkibia became a married woman, she gave
the holy veil of her hair to Queen Hera.

34   ON THE DAUGHTER OF LYKAMBES
      I pray for one gift: that I might merely touch
      Neoboule's hand.

35   LOVE
      I live here miserable and broken with desire,
      pierced through to the bones by the bitterness
      of this god-given painful love.

      O comrade, this passion makes my limbs limp
      and tramples over me.

36   THIRST
      I want to fight you
      just as when I am thirsty I want to drink.

37   ON A HANGING
      They hung their heads to one side, choking,
      and disgorged their remaining arrogance.

38   QUALITY IN LOVE
      How can I like the way she makes love?
      Give me sweet figs before sour wild pears.

39   OLD AGE
      A life of doing nothing is good for old men,
      especially if they are simple in their ways,
      or stupid, or inane in their endless blabber
      as old men tend to be.

40   PERIKLES THE GUEST
                    Like the Mykonians, Perikles,
                        you drink our unmixed wine
      and pay for nothing.

You broke into this party, uninvited, and act as if
    among old friends.
Your stomach has tricked the brains in your skull
    and now you are shameless.

41   ON THE PEOPLE'S CENSURE

No man, Aisimides, who bows to the mud-slinging
    mob has ever been capable of profound
    pleasures.

42   ON WRONGDOERS

                One big thing I understand:
I know how to spit back with black venom
against the man who wrongs me.

43   THE ROBE

Your telltale robe is bulging, you poor tramp,
and the men you love sit beside you.
The ditchdigger is in on your fancy story
and so is your husband Ariphantos.
Lucky Ariphantos didn't catch the fumes
of that stinking billygoat thief,
for while he was staving off the potter
    Aischylides,
the digger dug out your cherry,
and now your swollen belly tells the tale.

44   AFTER THE DROWNING
    OF HIS SISTER'S HUSBAND

Now, I have no desire for poetry or joy,
yet I will make nothing better by crying,
nor worse by seeking good foods and pleasure.

45   MODERATION

O my soul, my soul—you are mutilated helplessly
by this blade of sorrow. Yet rise and bare your
    chest,
face those who would attack you, be strong, give no
    ground.
And if you defeat them, do not brag like a loud-
    mouth,
nor, if they beat you, run home and lie down to cry.
Keep some measure in your joy—or in your
    sadness during
crisis—that you may understand man's up-and-
    down life.

46   ON THE DEATH OF TWO FRIENDS*

Broad earth, now you entomb Megatimos and
    Aristophon
    who were the two tall columns of this island
    Naxos.

47   ON A LEWD SERVANT

And wandering about the household
was that hateful chattering eunuch.

48   PERIKLES TO ELPINIKE

Lady, you are much too old
to rub yourself with perfume.

49   AN ANIMAL APPEALS TO ZEUS†

O father Zeus, you who control the cosmos, and
    oversee the actions of man,
his criminal and lawful acts, you also judge the
    arrogance and trial of wild beasts.

* Ascription to Archilochos is uncertain.
† Probably a fox.

50   JUSTICE
My lord Apollo, single out the guilty ones,
and in your customary way, destroy them all.

51   PERFUME
                    Her breasts and her dark hair
were perfume, and even an old man would love her.

52   TO A GIRLFRIEND'S FATHER
Father Lykambes, what is this new silliness?
                    Are your natural brains
gone wholly bad? The neighbors laugh openly
                    at your absurd life,
and you persist in chattering like a cricket.

53   ON DROWNED BODIES
Let us hide the dreadful
gifts of lord Poseidon.

54   DEATH
When dead no man finds respect or glory from men
of his town. Rather, we hope while alive for some
favor from the living. The dead are always scorned.

Kallinos

*The content of the fragments indicates that
Kallinos was active roughly in the middle of the
seventh century B.C. The Cimmerians were barbarians
from the Crimea and Southern Russia who for a
time threatened to overwhelm parts of Asia Minor,
including the Greek cities of the coast. Kallinos lived
in Ephesos, one of these cities. The surviving
fragments—like those of Tyrtaios—show essentially
an adaptation of Homeric style and language to the
demands of the present (as if one were to create
war propaganda from the King James Version of the
Old Testament prophets). The only major change
from Homer is the exclusive focus on courage as
sacrificial patriotism rather than a means chiefly for
the acquisition of individual glory. All the fragments
are elegiac.*

(On Elegy)   Among the best writers in this meter
Proklos includes Kallinos of Ephesos, Mimnermos of
Kolophon, and also Philetas the son of Telephos,
from Kos, and Kallimachos the son of Battos.

PHOTIOS, Library

55   A CALL TO ARMS AGAINST THE
     CIMMERIAN INVADERS
When will you show some courage, young
   comrades?
How long will you lie back and do nothing?
Lazing in shabby peace on our land bled by war,
have you no shame before the neighboring
   townsmen?

Let each man hurl his spear once more before he
   dies,
for glory dazzles on our helmets when we battle

the enemy for farmland and children and true wife.
Death will come only when the web of destiny
is spun.
    So move out, charge into the barbarous ranks
with spear held high and shield gripping a brave
    heart.
From death there is no escape; all men face the
    dark,
even those with blood of gods in their veins.

Often a man flees from the clash and thud of
    spears
and comes home to fall into sudden doom,
but he is neither loved nor missed by his
    townsmen.

Yet when a hero dies the great and small shed
    tears;
by a whole people a brave warrior is mourned.
In life he seems a demigod before the crowd;
as a marble pillar they look upon his strength,
for all alone he does the great deeds of an army.

56   TO ZEUS

Pity the people of Smyrna,
and now recall
if they ever burned for you
the choice thighs of oxen.

Tyrtaios

*Tyrtaios was active at Sparta during the Second
Messenian War, that is, some time in the seventh
century B.C. The legend that he came originally from
Athens seems to be false. His works included
marching songs (now lost) and elegies. In the
remains of the latter, martial exhortations
predominate, as with Kallinos. And like Kallinos,
Tyrtaios modifies the Homeric tradition in the
direction of a more corporate and collective ethos.
He came at the time of Sparta's transition from an
ordinary Greek city to a severely disciplined military
commune.*

The Spartans swore that they would take Messene or
die themselves. When the oracle told them to take
an Athenian general, they chose Tyrtaios, the lame
poet, who rekindled their courage, and he took
Messene in the twentieth year of the war.

The *Suda Lexicon*

And Philochoros says that when the Spartans
overpowered the Messenians through the generalship
of Tyrtaios, they made it a custom of their military
expeditions that after the evening meal when the
paean had been sung each man would sing a poem
by Tyrtaios, and the leader would judge the singing
and give the winner a prize of meat.

ATHENAIOS, *Doctors at Dinner*

❖❖❖❖❖❖❖❖❖❖❖❖❖❖❖❖❖❖❖❖❖❖❖❖❖❖❖

57   SPARTAN SOLDIER

It is beautiful when a brave man of the front ranks
    falls and dies, battling for his homeland,
and ghastly when a man flees planted fields and
    city
    and wanders begging with his dear mother,
aging father, little children and true wife.

[39]

He will be scorned in every new village,
reduced to want and loathsome poverty; and shame
    will brand his family line, his noble
figure. Derision and disaster will hound him.
    A turncoat gets no respect or pity;
so let us battle for our country and freely give
    our lives to save our darling children.
Young men, fight shield to shield and never
        succumb
    to panic or miserable flight,
but steel the heart in your chests with
        magnificence
    and courage. Forget your own life
when you grapple with the enemy. Never run
    and let an old soldier collapse
whose legs have lost their power. It is shocking
        when
    an old man lies on the front line
before a youth: an old warrior whose head is white
    and beard gray, exhaling his strong soul
into the dust, clutching his bloody genitals
    in his hands: an abominable vision,
foul to see: his flesh naked. But in a young man
    all is beautiful when he still
possesses the shining flower of lovely youth.
    Alive he is adored by men,
desired by women, and finest to look upon
    when he falls dead in the forward clash.
Let each man spread his legs, rooting them in the
        ground,
    bite his teeth into his lips, and hold.

58   FRONTIERS
You should reach the limits of virtue
before you cross the border of death.

Semonides

Born on Samos, Semonides may have become
associated with the island of Amorgos as leader of a
colony there. He probably was active in the second
half of the seventh century B.C. *His works included*
iambic poems (a rather long satire on women is
extant) and two books of elegies. In the iambics his
language is Ionic.

In his response to the experience of human
subjection to the gods (a topic particularly
characteristic of the Lyric Age) Semonides differs
from Archilochos. The earlier poet had concluded
upon a fusion of activism and resignation. But
Semonides deduced instead a code of passivity and
hedonism.

Amorgos is one of the Sporades islands and was the
home of the iambic poet Semonides.

STRABON, *Geography*

Semonides, son of Krines, from Amorgos, writer of
iambic verse. Originally he was from Samos but
during the colonization of Amorgos he was sent by
the Samians as a leader. He built three cities in
Amorgos: Minoa, Aigialos and Arkesime. He lived
390 years after the Trojan War. According to some,
he was the first to write iambic verse, and he wrote
the *History of the Samians* in two books of elegiac
verse, and other diverse poetry.

The *Suda Lexicon*

I know that you have lived a thousand things worthy
of iambic satire, and so bad that even Archilochos
himself could not stand to write about even one of
your outrageous acts, even if he called in as
collaborators Hipponax and Semonides.

LOUKIANOS, *The Liar*

◇◆◇◆◇◆◇◆◇◆◇◆◇◆◇◆◇◆◇◆◇◆◇◆◇◆◇

59   THE DARKNESS OF HUMAN LIFE

My child, deep-thundering Zeus controls the end
of all that is, disposing as he wills.
We who are mortals have no mind; we live like
        cattle,
day to day, knowing nothing of god's plans
to end each one of us. Yet we are fed
by hope and faith to dream impossible plans.
Some wait for a day to come, others watch
the turning of years. No one among the mortals
feels so broken as not to hope in coming time
to fly home rich to splendid goods and lands.
Yet before he makes his goal, odious old age
lays hold of him first. Appalling disease
consumes another. Some are killed in war
where death carries them under the dark earth.
Some drown and die under the myriad waves
when a hurricane slams across the blue salt water
cracking their cargo ship. Others rope a noose
around their wretched necks and choose to die,
abandoning the sun of day. A thousand black
        spirits
waylay man with unending grief and suffering.
If you listen to my counsel, you won't want
the good things of life; nor batter your heart
by torturing your skull with cold remorse.

60   LIFE AND DEATH

Later we will have a long time to lie dead
yet the few years we have now we live badly.

61   REMEMBRANCE OF THE DEAD

If we were sensible we would not spend
more than a day of sorrow for the dead.

62   ON MATRIMONY

Man gets nothing brighter than a kind wife
and nothing more chilling than a bad hag.

[42]

63   BREVITY OF LIFE*

One verse by the blind poet of Chios is indelible:
"The life of man is like a summer's leaf."
Yet few who hear these words take them into their
        heart,
for hope is rooted in every youthful soul,
the lovely flower of youth grows tall with color,
life will have no end,
or there is no place for growing old, for death;
and while in health, no fear of foul disease.
Poor fools! in islands of illusion,
for men have but a day of youth and life.
You few who understand, know when death is near
the food you give your soul must be supreme.

* Ascribed by Edmonds to Semonides. The "blind poet" is Homer.

Terpandros

Traditionally regarded as the first to make the choral lyric a developed art form, Terpandros was a fellow countryman of Alkaios and Sappho. But he was earlier by about a generation (his period of activity was the middle of the seventh century B.C.) and seems to have worked chiefly at Sparta, where he only briefly preceded Alkman. He is credited with increasing the strings of the lyre from four to seven. No fragments survive whose authenticity is uncontested.

Furthermore, Pindar claims that Terpandros was the inventor of *skolia* (drinking) songs.

Music was first established in Sparta by Terpandros.
PLUTARCH, On Music

The Spartans were fighting among themselves and sent to Lesbos for the musician Terpandros; he came and made their minds tranquil and stopped the quarrel. After that whenever the Spartans listened to a musician, they would say, "He is not the equal of the poet of Lesbos."
The Suda Lexicon

64 HYMN TO ZEUS
Zeus, inceptor of all,
of all things the commander,
Zeus, I bring you this gift:
the beginning of song.

65 TO APOLLO AND THE MUSES

Let us pour a libation
to the Muses, daughters
of Memory, and to Leto's
son, their lord Apollo.

66 SPARTA

The Muse sings brilliantly and
spears of young men flower.
Justice, defender of brave works,
goes down the street of light.

Alkman

*The first fully visible representative of the choral
ode lived at Sparta, and was active probably during
the middle of the seventh century B.C. It is possible
that he was (like several other poets of his time)
brought in from the East—in Alkman's case, from
Sardis in Lydia (Asia Minor).*

*His works were arranged in six books. They
included* partheneia, hymns *and* prooimia *(hexameter
preludes to recitations of epic poetry). His language
is strongly Doric, with Aiolic and Homeric influences.*

*Alkman in his fragments seems a poet of wayward
and playful sensitivity. The long and difficult
fragment of a* partheneion *("Song for a Choir of
Virgins") illustrates this sensitivity in the vivid,
glancing personal references, while "Rest" and
"Lakonian Wine" may serve to show its range in
nature and conviviality.*

Do not judge the man by the gravestone. The tomb
you see is small but it holds the bones of a great
man. For know that this is Alkman, supreme artist
of the Lakonian lyre, who commanded the nine
Muses. And twin continents dispute whether he is of
Lydia or Lakonia, for the mothers of a singer are
many.

ANTIPATROS OF THESSALONIKE

67 ARS POETICA
I know the tunes
of every bird,

but I, Alkman, found my words and song
in the tongue
of the strident partridge.

68   REST

Now chasms and mountain summits are asleep,
and sierra slopes and ravines;
creeping things nourished by the dark earth,
hillside beasts and generations of bees,
monsters in the depths of the purple brine,
all lie asleep,
and also tribes of flying birds.

69   ON THE FEATS OF A YOUNG GIRL

Often at night along the mountain tops,
when gods are reveling by torch light,
you came carrying a great jar
(like one shepherds use) but of heavy gold.
You filled the jar with milk
drawn from a lioness, and made a great cheese
unbroken and gleaming white.

70   ON THE WORM

The dappled worm is the murderer
within the eye of blooming vines.

71   IN MYTHOLOGY

Dew, a child of moon and air,
causes the deergrass to grow.

72   SONG FOR A CHOIR OF VIRGINS*

THE WHOLE CHOIR

There is a vengeance from the gods,
but happy is the man who weaves
the fabric of his days with peace,
and without tears.

* The choir consists of ten virgins. The half-choirs speak in the first
person singular, in friendly rivalry, each praising its own half-choir
leaders.

AGIDO'S HALF-CHOIR

But I sing
of Agido's light. I see her
like the sun who shines on us
by order of Agido.

HAGESICHORA'S HALF-CHOIR

Our splendid
leader will not have us praise
or abuse her, for her brilliance
is as if among a herd of cattle
one had set a champion racehorse,
sinewy, strong, with thunder-ringing hooves,
a creature from a dream with wings.
Do you see? The horse is Venetian,
and the mane of our cousin
Hagesichora is a blossom
of the purest gold,
and below is her silver face.
Can I tell you this more clearly?
There you have Hagesichora.
In beauty she may be second to Agido
but she will run like a
Skythian horse against a Lydian racer.
For as we carry Orthria's plow
so the Pleiades of dawn will rise
and strive against us
like the burning star of Sirios
through the ambrosial night.

AGIDO'S HALF-CHOIR

All our wealth of purple dye
or the dappled snake of full gold
about our wrist or our Lydian
wimple that is the sweet glory
of all these tender-eyed girls,
no, nothing will keep them off.
Not Nanno's soft braids,
nor Areta's godlike beauty,
neither Thylakis nor Kleësisera.

HAGESICHORA'S HALF-CHOIR

You need not go to Ainesimbrota
and say: let Astaphis be mine,
have Philylla look my way,
and Damareta and darling Ianthemis.
For Hagesichora is our saviour.
Is Hagesichora of the lovely
ankles not right here with us?

AGIDO'S HALF-CHOIR

Yes, she waits by our Agido,
and commends our ceremonies.
O gods, receive our prayers,
for you determine everything
accomplished. My choir leader,
I tell you I a girl shrieked
in vain like an owl
from the roof tops.

HAGESICHORA'S HALF-CHOIR

                But my great wish
is to please the Lady of the Dawn
who has healed our sore wounds.
Only Hagesichora could give
her girls the peace they desired.

THE WHOLE CHOIR

A great chariot simply follows
the course of its trace-horse;
in a vessel all must swiftly
heed the shouting of the helmsman,
so our combined choir may not
sing more sweetly than the Sirens—
for they are gods—but how we sang,
we ten girls with even one away!
And her song is like a swan
by the Xanthos river, and she
with the splendor of her blond hair.

73   SUPPLICATION
      The girls fell to their knees, helpless—
      like small birds under a hovering hawk.

74   HOME OF THE NORTH WIND
      The Rhipé mountain flowering with forests
      is the breast of black-flowing night.

75   TO THE DIOSKOUROI
      Kastor and noble Polydeukes, you trainers
      of swift stallions, are extraordinary horsemen.

76   TO HERA
      I pray to you, Hera,
      and bring you as my offering
      a delicate garland of marigold
      and galingale.

77   ON THE POET ALKMAN
      He is no boorish farmer or
      a clumsy pigkeeper or even
      a sheep-chaser. He was not born
      in Thessaly or Erysiche
      but in Sardis on the high hills.

78   ON A POETESS
      Aphrodite commands and love rains
      upon my body and melts my heart

      for Megalostrata to whom the sweet
      Muse gave the gift of poetry. O
      happy girl of the goldenrod hair!

79 ALKMAN'S SUPPER

Get him that enormous caldron on the tripod
so he can bloat his stomach with every food.
It is cool but soon will boil with good soup
which gobbler Alkman likes sparkling hot,
especially in the cold season of the solstice.
The glutton Alkman abstains from fancy dishes
but like the demos eats a plain massive meal.

80 WEDDING FEAST

Seven couches and as many tables
spread with poppy cakes and linseed and
sesame, and among the wooden flagons
were honey cakes for the young.

81 THE FOUR SEASONS

Three seasons were created: summer
and winter and a third in autumn,
and even a fourth—the spring—
when the fields are heavy with crops
and a glutton still goes hungry.

82 LAKONIAN WINE

I know the wine from the Five Hills,
wine from Oinos or Denthiades
or Karystos or wine of Onogla
or Stathmi—unboiled, unfired wines
of fine aroma.

83 ON THE KALCHA FLOWER

She wears a gold chain
made from slender petals
of purple kalcha flowers.

84   THE JOURNEY
      Narrow is our way of life
      and necessity is pitiless.

85   ON TANTALOS
      The guilty man sat
      among pleasant things under a hanging rock,
      and from his chair he looked
      and then the vision faded.

86   APHRODITE
      You are from the beautiful island Kypros
      and from the sea-surrounded city Paphos.

87   WANDERING LOVE
      It is not Aphrodite but riotous Eros who is
      playing like a child,
      scuttling down across the tips of meadow ferns.
      Please, do not crush them.

88   TO THE MOON GODDESS
      I am your servant, Artemis.

      You draw your long bow at night,
      clothed in the skins of wild beasts.

      Now hear our beautiful singing.

89   I AM OLD
      O girls of honey-sweet voices, my limbs are weak.
      They will not bear me. I wish, ah, I wish I were
      a carefree kingfisher flying over flowering foam
      with the halcyons—sea-blue holy birds of spring.

90   MAN'S LESSONS
      Experience and suffering
      are the mother of wisdom.

91   ON HIS POETRY
      Muse of the round sky, daughter of Zeus,
      I sing my poems loud and clear to you.

92   WINDFLOWER
      Bright-shining.

93   CALM SEA
      The calm sea falls dumbly
      on the shore
      among a tangle of seaweed.

Alkaios

Alkaios' poetry is deeply involved in his political
vicissitudes. The greater part of his life was spent in
fighting reform movements which shook the
established aristocracy of his native island Lesbos.
He was born around 630 B.C. Some twenty years later
the reigning tyrant, Melanchros, was overthrown by
Pittakos and the brothers of Alkaios. Alkaios was
for a time involved in the alliance with Pittakos,
and even fought with him against the Athenians at
Sigeion (near Troy). But a break came, and Pittakos
allied himself with Myrsilos to govern Mytilene
while Alkaios went into exile at Pyrrha (another
town on Lesbos). At the death of Myrsilos, Alkaios
returned home but was soon in exile again, this time
apparently traveling widely, as far as Egypt. (His
brother served in the army of Babylon under
Nebuchadnezzar, in campaigns which led to the
capture of Jerusalem, 597 B.C.) Some time after 590
B.C. Pittakos forgave Alkaios, and the latter probably
returned home.

Alkaios' works consisted of at least ten books,
chiefly monodic. Hymns, political, erotic and
sympotic poems predominate. He wrote in the Aiolic
dialect, in a direct and emphatic style.

In his political poems Alkaios shows considerable
similarity to Theognis. Both were hard-core
aristocrats, convinced of the superiority of their
class and cause, identifying private values with
public right. (Alkaios seems to have gone so far as to
support revolution against the established
government.)

The influence of Alkaios is probably most seen in
three places: the appropriations of Alkaios' forms
and subjects by Horace; the recurrent metaphor (in
poetry and elsewhere) of the "ship of state"; and
the convivial poem (compare "Winter Evening" with
Horace, Odes I, 9, and Milton, Sonnet XX).

Alkaios is rightly awarded the golden quill in that
part of his work where he assails tyrants; his ethical

value is also great; his style is concise, magnificent,
exact, very much like Homer's; but he stoops to
humor and love when better suited for higher themes.

QUINTILIAN

94 INSTANT
I already hear the flowering spring.

95 PRAYER TO THE CONSTELLATION
DIOSKOUROI, PATRON DEITIES OF
MARINERS
Come with me now and leave the land of
Pelops, mighty sons of Zeus and Leda,
and in kindness spread your light on us,
Kastor and Polydeukes.

You who wander above the long earth
and over all the seas on swift horses,
easily delivering mariners
from pitiful death,

fly to the masthead of our swift ship,
and gazing over foremast and forestays,
light a clear path through the midnight gloom
for our black vessel.

96 WINTER EVENING
Zeus rumbles and a mammoth winter of snow
pours from the sky; agile rivers are ice.

Damn the winter cold! Pile up the burning logs
and water the great flagons of red wine;
place feather pillows by your head, and drink.

Let us not brood about hard times. Bakchos,
our solace is in *you* and your red wines:
our medicine of grape. Drink deeply, drink.

97   SUMMER STAR

Wash your gullet with wine for the Dog-Star
    returns
with the heat of summer searing a thirsting earth.
Cicadas cry softly under high leaves, and pour
    down
shrill song incessantly from under their wings.
The artichoke blooms, and women are warm and
    wanton—
but men turn lean and limp for the burning Dog-
              Star parches their brains and knees.

98   WHY WAIT FOR THE LIGHTING
      OF THE LAMPS?

Let us drink. Why wait for the lighting of the
    lamps?
Night is a hair's breadth away. Take down the great
    goblets
from the shelf, dear friend, for the son of Semele
    and Zeus
gave us wine to forget our pains. Mix two parts
    water, one wine,
and let us empty the dripping cups—urgently.

99   DRINK, SONG AND SHIPS

Why water more wine in the great bowl?
Why do you drown your gullet in grape?
I cannot let you spill out your life
on song and drink. Let us go to sea,

and not let the wintry calm of morning
slip by as a drunken sleep. Had we
boarded at dawn, seized rudder and spun
the flapping cross-jack into the wind,

we would be happy now, happy as swimming
in grape. But you draped a lazy arm
on my shoulder, saying: "Sir, a pillow,
your singing does not lead me to ships."

100   COSTUME
But let them hang braided garlands
of yellow dill around our necks,
and drape strands of redolent myrrh
across our breasts.

101   ON HIS BROTHER'S HOMECOMING
You have come home from the ends of the earth,
Antimenidas, my dear brother; come
with a gold and ivory handle to your sword.
You fought alongside the Babylonians
and your prowess saved them from annihilation
when you battled and cut down a warrior giant
who was almost eight feet tall.

102   THE LYRE
Daughter of the rock and the gray sea,
                        you fill all hearts
with triumph, tortoise shell of the sea.

103   BIRDS
                        What birds are these
wildgeese—flying from precincts where the earth
                        and oceans end—
with their enormous wings and speckled throats?

104   ON MONEY
Aristodemos wasn't lying
when he said one day in Sparta,

"Money is the man; and a poor man
can be neither good nor honorable."

105   TO THE RIVER HEBROS

Hebros, most beautiful river near Ainos,
you carry a shining bath of Thracian foam
out into the purple sea. And many girls
                stand near you,

and with soft hands rub oil on the smooth flesh
of their beautiful thighs. And they pour
your water over themselves like a sooth-
                ing unguent.

106   HELEN AND THETIS

Helen, your sinful deeds brought a bitter end
to Priam and his lovely children. They say
because of you holy Ilium was destroyed
                by climbing fire.

But the son of Aiakos did not find such a wife
when he summoned the blessed gods to his wedding
and took the delicate sea-nymph Thetis from
                the watery palace

of Nereus, bringing her to the mountain cave
of the centaur Cheiron. There, the love of Peleus
for his sea-nymph led him to lie naked with
                the untouched virgin,

and within the year she bore a son, Achilles;
bravest demigod and splendid driver of
tawny stallions. But for Helen, Ilium and
                her people were destroyed.

107   HYMN TO APOLLO*

Our king Apollo, O child of mighty Zeus,
when you were born your father gave you
a gold headband and a lyre of tortoise shell,
and more: a chariot drawn by swans. You were

* Text is derived from a paraphrase of Alkaios' poem.

[58]

to go to Delphi and the Kastalian springs
whose waters are the gift of broad Kephissos,
and there deliver justice to the Hellenes
through the oracles. But when you seized the reins,

you made the swans sail north to the distant land
of the Hyperboreans, and though the Delphians
begged you to return—with paeans of flutes
and circles of girls dancing about the tripod—

Apollo, you remained to rule that people
through the long year. Came the season when the
     tripod
rings loud and clear in Delphi, you turned the swans
to Parnassos. It was high noon of summer

when you glided back from the far northlands;
swallows and nightingales were singing; cicadas
also sang about you; silver brooks poured down
from Kastalia, and the great river Kephissos

threw blue-foaming waves into the bright wind:
     yes,
even the waters knew a god was coming home.

108   THE PEOPLE'S SICKNESS
       Poverty—our painful and uncontrolled disease—
       you maim great peoples with your sister
          Helplessness.

109   A WOMAN*
       Bad,
       every misery and disaster I've known, a woman

       with a home
       of shameful death,

* Very fragmentary text but not reconstructed.

[59]

incurable decrepitude coming on
and madness in the terrorized heart of the stag,

out of his mind
and ruined.

110   THINGS OF WAR
The great house glitters with bronze. War has pat-
            terned the roof with shining helmets,
their horsehair plumes waving in wind, headdress
            of fighting men. And pegs
are concealed under bright greaves of brass which
            block the iron-tipped arrows. Many
fresh-linen corslets are hanging and hollow shields
            are heaped about the floor,
and standing in rows are swords of Chalkidian steel,
            belt-knives and warriors' kilts.
We cannot forget our arms and armor when soon
            our dreadful duties begin.

111   WALLS AND THE CITY
Not homes with beautiful roofs,
nor walls of permanent stone,
nor canals and piers for ships

make the city—but men of strength.

Not stone and timber, nor skill
of carpenter—but men brave
who will handle sword and spear.

With these you have: city and walls.

112   HYPOCRISY
Father Zeus, in our worst moment of hardship,
the Lydians selflessly gave us two thousand
staters, and gave us hope that we might re-enter
                our sacred city

of Mytilene. There we were only strangers,
but in our own homeland the cunning fox
made honeyed speeches for the blackmail gold,
                    and then betrayed us.

113   ON PREMATURE POLITICAL ACTIVITY
It is late; for the harvest is in.
Before, we hoped that the full vines
would bring a plenitude of fine grapes,
but the clusters are slow
to ripen and the landlords
picked unripe bunches from the branch.
We have many grapes now—green and sour.

114   ON THE TYRANT PITTAKOS
                    One and all,
you have proclaimed Pittakos, the lowborn,
to be tyrant of your lifeless and doomed
land. Moreover, you deafen him with praise.

115   A NATION AT SEA
I can't tell you which way the gale has turned
for waves crash in from west and east, and we
are tossed and driven between, our black ship
            laboring under the giant storm.

The sea washes across the decks and maststep
and dark daylight already shows through long rents
in the sails. Even the halyards slacken as
            windward waves coil above the hull.

What sore labor to bale the water we've shipped!
Let us raise bulwarks and ride out the storm,
heeding my words: "Let each man now be famous."
            Yet base cowards betray the state.

116   TO THE MYTILENIANS
                          The local tyrant
rants and blusters and you are silenced
like a school of frightened neophytes
confronting the dead in holy rituals.

But I tell you, O citizens of Lesbos,
rise up and quench the smoldering logs
before their flames climb and consume you all
in total fire!

117   EARTHQUAKE
The tyrant's craze for absolute power will soon
demolish his country; already the earth trembles.

118   TO THE BASEBORN TYRANT
I say this to him too: he is a strident
lute who would like to be heard at a party
of the well-born people of Lesbos. Better
had he chosen to drink with the filthy herd.
He married a daughter from the ancient
race of Atreus; now let him offend our people
as he did the former tyrant Myrsilos,
until the Wargod makes us revolt. We must
forget our anger and cease these pitiful
clashes between brothers. Only a god
could have maddened our people into war
and so give Pittakos his bit of glory.

119   TO HIS FRIEND MELANIPPOS
Drink and be drunk with me, Melanippos. Do you
think when you have crossed the great fuming
    river,
you will ever return from Hell to see the clean
bright light of the sun? Do not strive for wild
    hopes.

Even the son of Aiolos, King Sisyphos, wisest of
    men,
thought he had eluded death. But for all his brains

Fate made him recross Acheron, and the son of
    Kronos
assigned him a terrible trial below the dark earth.

Come, I beg you not to brood about these hopeless
matters while we are young. We will suffer what
    must

be suffered. When the wind is waiting in the north,
a good captain will not swing into the open sea.

Sappho

Sappho was the compatriot and approximate
contemporary of Alkaios. Her home on Lesbos was
at Mytilene. She came of a noble family. The names
of some of her family have been preserved:
Skamandronymos was her father, Kleïs her mother.
Her husband was Kerkylas of Andros, and she
named her daughter Kleïs for her mother. One of her
brothers was Charaxos. Political changes led to her
exile (with other members of the aristocracy) around
600 B.C. She spent some time in Sicily before she was
allowed to return home.

Her chief concerns, apparently, were with personal
relationships, and these above all among a circle of
girls of the upper class. Among those whom she
loved were Atthis and Anaktoria. We hear also the
names of several rivals: Andromeda and Gorgo.
Fittingly, the goddess whom she affectionately
worshiped was Aphrodite. Indeed the connection
between life and religion was so close for Sappho
that she might have repeated the words of Eranna
in Rilke's poem:

> . . . denn die schöne Göttin in der Mitte
> ihrer Mythen glüht und lebt mein Leben.

> (for the fair goddess amid her myths glows
> and lives my life)

The story that Sappho loved a certain Phaon and
died by leaping from the Leukadian rock for love of
him resulted probably from a misunderstanding of a
ritual dirge for the vegetation god Phaon.

In appearance she is said to have been small and
dark.

The works of Sappho were arranged in seven
books, the seventh comprising wedding songs. They
survived into Byzantine times, but were then
probably destroyed by Christian intolerance.

There seems to be a slight difference in style
between some works of Sappho which may have

been written for a more public audience (e.g.,
the "Wedding of Andromache") and the poems
which are more private and personal in character.
The former show an inclination to admit Homeric
forms and prosody; the latter are purely in the
Aiolic dialect. The intense power of her simple and
euphonious style has been remarked upon from the
ancient critics until now.

In her outlook Sappho is notable, among other
things, for her interpretation of love: unlike many
of the poets of the Lyric Age, she regarded love not
as a dangerous obsession, but as fulfillment. And
she elevated love into the criterion of value
("To Anaktoria").

Her influence on later literature, whether in style
or subject, has been considerable. One could start
with the following: Catullus LI, Ovid's Sappho
Phaoni in the Heroides, plays by Grillparzer and
Durrell, Rilke's Sappho poems in Neue Gedichte, and
the poems of H.D.

Some say nine Muses—but count again.
Behold the tenth: Sappho of Lesbos.

PLATO

A contemporary of Pittakos and Alkaios was Sappho
—a marvel. In all the centuries since history began
we know of no woman who in any true sense can
be said to rival her as a poet.

STRABON, *Geography*

120   THE LYRIC POEM

Come, holy tortoise shell,
my lyre, and become a poem.

121   NOW I BEGIN

I begin with words of air
yet they are good to hear.

[65]

122   HEADDRESS
My mother always said
that in her youth she was
exceedingly in fashion

wearing a purple ribbon
looped in her hair. But
the girl whose hair is yellower

than torchlight need wear no
colorful ribbons from Sardis—
but a garland of fresh flowers.

123   HER INNOCENCE
I do not have a rancorous spirit
but the simple heart of a child.

124   TO ANAKTORIA
Some say cavalry and others claim
infantry or a fleet of long oars
is the supreme sight on the black earth.
I say it is

the one you love. And easily proved.
Did not Helen—who far surpassed all
mortals in beauty—desert the best
of men, her king,

and sail off to Troy and forget
her daughter and dear kinsmen? Merely
the Kyprian's gaze made her bend and led
her from her path;

these things remind me now
of Anaktoria who is far,
and I
for one

[66]

would rather see her warm supple step
and the sparkle of her face—than watch
all the dazzling chariots and armored
                                    hoplites of Lydia.

125   ALONE*
The moon and Pleiades
are set. Midnight,
and time spins away.
I lie in bed, alone.

126   TO EROS
You burn me.

127   THE BLAST OF LOVE
Like a mountain whirlwind
punishing the oak trees,
love shattered my heart.

128   SEIZURE
To me he seems like a god
as he sits facing you and
hears you near as you speak
softly and laugh

in a sweet echo that jolts
the heart in my ribs. For now
as I look at you my voice
is empty and

can say nothing as my tongue
cracks and slender fire is quick
under my skin. My eyes are dead
to light, my ears

* Authorship uncertain.

pound, and sweat pours over me.
I convulse, paler than grass,
and feel my mind slip as I
go close to death.

129   WORLD
I could not hope
to touch the sky
with my two arms.

130   BEACH COLOR
The furzy flower of the golden broom
grew along the shore.

131   LET SLEEPING DOGS LIE
Don't stir up the small
heaps of beach jetsam.

132   TO HER GIRLFRIENDS
On this day I will sing beautifully
and make you happy, dear comrades.

133   FULL MOON
The glow and beauty of the stars
are nothing near the splendid moon
when in her roundness she burns silver
about the world.

134   THEN
In gold sandals
dawn like a thief
fell upon me.

135 THE CRICKET
When sun dazzles the earth
with straight-falling flames,
a cricket rubs its wings
scraping up a shrill song.

136 PIGEONS AT REST
The hearts in the pigeons grew cold
and their wings dropped to their sides.

137 THE HERALD
Nightingale, with your
lovely voice, you are
the herald of spring.

138 EVENING STAR
Of all stars Hesperos,
is the most beautiful.

139 CEREMONY
Now the earth with many flowers
puts on her spring embroidery.

140 DEAR ATTHIS, DID YOU KNOW?
In dream Love came out of heaven
and put on his purple cloak.

141 TO ATTHIS
My Atthis, although our dear Anaktoria
lives in distant Sardis,
she thinks of us constantly, and

of the life we shared in days when for her
you were a splendid goddess,
and your singing gave her deep joy.

Now she shines among Lydian women as
when the red-fingered moon
rises after sunset, erasing

stars around her, and pouring light equally
across the salt sea
and over densely flowered fields;

and lucent dew spreads on the earth to quicken
roses and fragile thyme
and the sweet-blooming honey-lotus.

Now while our darling wanders she remem-
bers lovely Atthis' love,
and longing sinks deep in her breast.

She cries loudly for us to come! We hear,
for the night's many tongues
carry her cry across the sea.

142   A LETTER*
"Sappho, if you do not come out,
I swear, I will love you no more.

O rise and free your lovely strength
from the bed and shine upon us.
Lift off your Chian nightgown, and

like a pure lily by a spring,
bathe in the water. Our Kleïs
will bring a saffron blouse and violet

tunic from your chest. We will place
a clean mantle on you, and crown
your hair with flowers. So come, darling,

with your beauty that maddens us,
and you, Praxinoa, roast the nuts
for our breakfast. One of the gods

* The speaker may be Atthis, whose words Sappho is quoting.

is good to us, for on this day
Sappho, most beautiful of women,
will come with us to the white city

of Mytilene, like a mother
among her daughters." Dearest Atthis,
can you now forget all those days?

143   TO HER FRIEND

Honestly I wish I were dead!
Although she too cried bitterly

when she left, and said to me,
"Ah, what a nightmare it is now.
Sappho, I swear I go unwillingly."

And I answered, "Go, and be happy.
But remember me, for surely you
know how we worshiped you. If not,

then I want to remind you of all
the exquisite days
we two shared; how

you took garlands of violets
and roses, and when by my side
you tied them round you in soft bands,

and you took many flowers
and flung them in loops
about your sapling throat,

how the air was rich in a scent
of queenly spices made of myrrh
you rubbed smoothly on your limbs,

and on soft beds, gently, your desire
for delicate girls
was satisfied,

[71]

and how there was no dance and no
holy shrine
we two did not share,

no sound,
no
grove."

144   TO ATTHIS

Love—bittersweet, irrepressible—
loosens my limbs and I tremble.

Yet, Atthis, you despise my being.
To chase Andromeda, you leave me.

145   TO ATTHIS

I loved you, Atthis, long ago,
when my girlhood was in full flower
and you were like a graceless child.

146   LONG DEPARTURE

Then I said to the elegant ladies:
"How you will remember when you are old
the glorious things we did in our youth!

We did many pure and beautiful things.
Now that you are leaving the city,
love's sharp pain encircles my heart."

147   A PRAYER TO APHRODITE

On your dazzling throne, Aphrodite,
sly eternal daughter of Zeus,
I beg you: do not crush me with grief,

but come to me now—as once
you heard my far cry, and yielded,
slipping from your father's house

to yoke the birds to your gold
chariot, and came. Handsome sparrows
brought you swiftly to the dark earth,

their wings whipping the middle sky.
Happy, with deathless lips, you smiled:
"What is wrong, why have you called me?

What does your mad heart desire?
Whom shall I make love you, Sappho,
who is turning her back on you?

Let her run away, soon she'll chase you;
refuse your gifts, soon she'll give them.
She will love you, though unwillingly."

Then come to me now and free me
from fearful agony. Labor
for my mad heart, and be my ally.

148   TO APHRODITE OF THE FLOWERS,
AT KNOSSOS

Leave Krete and come to this holy temple
where the graceful grove of apple trees
circles an altar smoking with frank-
      incense.

Here roses leave shadow on the ground
and cold springs babble through apple branches
where shuddering leaves pour down pro-
      found sleep.

In our meadow where horses graze
and wild flowers of spring blossom,
anise shoots fill the air with a-
      roma.

And here, Queen Aphrodite, pour
heavenly nectar into gold cups
and fill them gracefully with sud-
      den joy.

149   TO LADY HERA

Lady Hera, while I pray let your
graceful form appear, which came once
to the dazzling kings of the Atreidai
when they prayed.

The Atreidai accomplished many feats
first at Ilium, and then on the sea
on their voyage back, but could not
reach home again

before imploring you, Zeus of the winds
and Thyone's lovely child: Dionysos.
So be kind, as in former days,
and now help *me*.

150   PARALYSIS

Mother darling, I cannot work the loom
for sweet Kypris has almost crushed me,
broken me with love for a slender boy.

151   DESIRE

                        For I am
a slave of the Kypros-born,
who lays a net of trickery.

152   FROM APHRODITE

I tell you, Sappho,
love is my servant.

153   TO EROS

From all the offspring
of the earth and heaven
love is the most precious.

[74]

154   THE DEATH OF ADONIS

Our tender Adonis is dying, O Kythereia,
What can we do?
Beat on your breasts, my girls, and tear
your dresses.

155   LOVE TOKEN

Your face is shaded, Aphrodite,
with a kerchief of porphyry
color: a precious gift from Timas
of far Phokaia.

156   DIALOG

Kypros-born, in dream
we two were talking.

157   TO APHRODITE

For you, Aphrodite, I will burn
the savory fat of a white she-goat.
All this I will leave behind for you.

158   TO APHRODITE

Aphrodite with gold flowers in your hair,
I say if only
some other fate were mine!

159   HEKATE

Hekate, shining of gold,
handmaid to Aphrodite.

160   PEITHO (PERSUASION)

You are the daughter of Aphrodite:
you confuse us
and we mortals love.

161   TO THE GRACES
        O daughters of Zeus,
        come to me now,
        O graces of the pink arms.

162   TO THE GRACES AND MUSES
        Come, come now,
        tender Graces,
        and Muses of the splendid hair.

163   MAKING OF THE POEM
        Come to me now, O Muses.
        Leave your gold house.

164   THE MUSES
        To me they brought honor, for they
        gave me the secret of their craft.

165   SLEEP

        May you find sleep on a
        soft girlfriend's breast.

166   BECAUSE OF A RIVAL
        Sappho, why do you condemn
        the many joys of Aphrodite?

167   A RIVAL
        By now they've had
        their fill of Gorgo.

168 THE VIRGIN
Like a sweet apple reddening on the high
tip of the topmost branch and forgotten
by the pickers—no, beyond their reach.

Like a hyacinth crushed in the mountains
by shepherds; lying trampled on the earth
yet blooming purple.

169 SAPPHO'S EPITHET
The honey-voiced girls.

170 LOOPS OF FLOWERS
Girls ripe for marriage
were braiding flowers.

171 BRIDEGROOM
What are you, my lovely bridegroom?
You are most like a slender sapling.

172 WEDDING SONG
Groom, we virgins at your door
will pass the night singing of the love
between you and your bride. Her limbs
are like violets.

Wake and call out the young men
your friends, and you can walk the streets
and we shall sleep less tonight than
the bright nightingale.

173 TO HER FRIENDS AT DAWN
Come, my darling girls,
let us stop singing now
for soon it will be day.

174   SONG OF THE WEDDING BED
        Bride, warm with rose-
        colored love, brightest
        ornament of the Paphian,
        come to the bedroom now,
        enter the bed and play
        tenderly with your man.
        May the Evening Star
        lead you eagerly
        to that instant when you
        will gaze in wonder
        before the silver throne
        of Hera, queen of marriage.

175   SONG FOR THE BRIDE
        No girl who ever was,
        O groom, was like her.

176   AFTER THE CEREMONY
        Happy groom, the wedding took place
        and the girl you prayed for is yours.

        Now her charming face is warm with love.

        My bride, your body is a joy,
        your eyes soft as honey,
        and love pours its light
        on your perfect features.

        Using all her skill Aphrodite
        honored you.

177   A LANKY GROOM
        Raise the ceiling and sing
        Hymen!
        Have carpenters raise the roof.
        Hymen!
        The groom who will come in
        is tall like towering Ares.

178 DRINKS FOR THE GROOM

The wine bowl was full
with perfect ambrosia.
Hermes took up a jug to pour wine for the gods;
then all gripped their goblets,
spilled out libations,
and shouted lots of good luck
to the groom.

179 GOODBYE, BE HAPPY

Goodbye, be happy, bride and groom.

Be happy, bride and honored groom.

180 THE GUARD OUTSIDE THE BRIDAL
CHAMBER

The doorkeeper's feet are fourteen
yards long. Ten shoemakers used up
five oxhides to cobble each sandal.

181 SHALL I?

I do not know what to do:
I say yes—and then no.

182 ONE NIGHT

All the while, believe me, I prayed
our night would last twice as long.

183 DANCERS

While the full moon rose, young girls
took their place around the altar.

In old days Kretan girls danced
supplely around an altar of love,
crushing the soft flowering grass.

184   BRIDE

O beautiful, O charming bride,
now you play with gold Aphrodite
and the roseate-ankled
Graces.

185   LOSS

Virginity, virginity, when you leave me,
where do you go?

I am gone and never come back to you.
I never return.

186   REMORSE

Do I still long
for my virginity?

187   WEDDING OF ANDROMACHE

Kypros!
A herald came.
Idaos. Racing powerfully.

Of the rest of Asia. Imperishable glory! (He said:)
"From holy Thebe and the waters of Plakia,
graceful Andromache coming with the navy
over the salt sea. They come with armbands of gold
and purple gowns and odd trinkets of rare design
and countless silver jars and ivory pins."
So he spoke. And Priam sprang to his feet

and the glowing news went from friend to friend
through the wide city. Instantly the sons of Ilios
hitched the mules to their finely-wheeled chariots,
and a throng of wives and slender-ankled girls
climbed inside. Priam's daughters rode alone,
while young men led their horses under the cars.
Greatly.
Charioteers.

Like gods.
Holy.
They all set out for Ilium
in the confusion of sweet flutes and crashing
    cymbals,
and girls sang a loud heavenly song
whose wonderful echo
touched the sky.
Everywhere in the streets.
Bowls and chalices.

Myrrh and cassia and incense rode on the wind.
Old women sang happily
and all the men sang out with thrilling force,
calling on Paean, great archer, lord of the lyre,
and sang of Hektor and Andromache like gods.

188   TO HERSELF

Let the depths of my soul be dumb
for I cannot think up
a clarion song about Adonis,

for Aphrodite who staggers me
with shameful lust
has reduced me to dull silence,

and Persuasion (who maddens one),
from her gold vial
spills tangy nectar on my mind.

189   HOMECOMING

You came. And you did well to come.
I longed for you and you brought fire
to my heart, which burns high for you.

Welcome, darling, be blessed three times
for all the hours of our separation.

190   HER RIVAL'S PEDIGREE
A very bright good morning,
Andromeda—O daughter
from kings and sons of kings.

191   RIVAL
I have lost, and you, Andromeda,
have made an excellent exchange.

192   ANDROMEDA, WHAT NOW?
                    Can this farm girl
in farm-girl finery burn your heart?
She is even ignorant of the way
to lift her gown over her ankles.

193   A RING
Silly woman. Yes, it is a ring,
but really, don't be so proud.

194   THE GIRL-RUNNER HERO
I taught Hero from the island
of Gyara
how to run like a star.

195   ARES' STRENGTH
Ares lets everybody
know that he could
drag off Hephaistos
with his bare hands.

196   BEFORE THE MURDER
It seems untrue but
once Leto and Niobe
were devoted friends.

[82]

197   TO THE NIGHTINGALE'S SISTER
Why do you trouble me—Pandion's
daughter, swallow out of heaven?

198   MONEY AND VIRTUE
If you are rich but not good
you court calamity,
yet being both
                    you stand
at the happy top of the world.

199   TO AN UNEDUCATED WOMAN
When dead you will lie forever forgotten,
for you have no claim to the Pierian roses.
Dim here, you will move more dimly in Hell,
flitting among the undistinguished dead.

200   TO A HANDSOME MAN
Stand up and gaze on me as friend
to friend. I ask you to reveal
the naked beauty of your eyes.

201   CONVERSATION WITH ALKAIOS
            Alkaios
Violet-haired, pure, honey-smiling Sappho,
I want to speak to you but shame disarms me.*

            Sappho
If you cared for what is upright and good,
and your tongue were not concocting trouble,
shame would not be hiding in your eyes
and you would speak out your real desires.

* Line 1, or lines 1 and 2, are ascribed to Alkaios.

202   APPEARANCES
       A handsome man now looks handsome.
       A good man will soon take on beauty.

203   RETURN
       O Gongyla, my darling rose,
       put on your milk-white gown. I want
       you to come back quickly. For my
       desire feeds on

       your beauty. Each time I see your gown
       I am made weak and happy. I too
       blamed the Kyprian. Now I pray
       she will not seek

       revenge, but may she soon allow
       you, Gongyla, to come to me
       again: you whom of all women
       I most desire.

204   UNGIVEN LOVE
       I am dry with longing
       and I hunger for her.

205   IN TIME OF STORM*
       When seastorms scream across the water,
       the sailor, fearing these wild blasts,
       spills his cargo overboard and veers
                            his vessel shoreward.

       I pray that I may be bound nowhere
       in time of storm, yet let my heart
       not cast her cargo fearfully
                            into the salt depths,

* Greek text of poem is largely reconstructed (invented) by Edmonds.

and let Nereus, with all the proper
ocean ceremonies, receive
                          the gift of my goods.

206   ART
      No girl I think will ever outshine
      your skill—no girl who will ever
      look into sunlight.

207   A CHILD OF GOD
      Gold is a child of God.
      Moths and worms
      do not eat it.
                   Gold overpowers
      a man's heart,
      even of the strongest man.

208   ASIAN DYES
      Her gay embroidered gown
      draped down to her toes:
      fine needlework from Lydia.

209   ON AMORGINE FABRICS
      She wore around her the soft
      fine linen robes of Amorgos.

210   JASON'S CLOTHING
      His cloak was of a cloth
      handspun from many colors.

211   WHEN YOU COME
      You will lie down and
      I shall lay out soft
      pillows for your body.

212   COMPARISONS
Softer than fine robes.

More golden than gold.

Sweeter than the lyre.

Far whiter than an egg.

213   THE PREEMINENCE OF LESBIAN POETRY
Towering over all lands
is the singer of Lesbos.

214   TO DIKA, NOT TO GO BAREHEADED
Dika, take some shoots of dill, and loop
them skillfully about your lovely hair.
The happy Graces love her who wears flowers
but turn their back on one who goes plain.

215   THE BEAUTY OF HER GIRLS
Mnasidika has a lovelier body
than even our soft Gyrinno's.

216   YIELDING
No more. Do not try
to bend a hard heart.

217   TRIAL
When anger floods into my chest,
I bite my tongue—not to explode.

218   BECAUSE OF THE PUNISHMENT
Tears came to the eyes
of even the holy gods.

219   A VISION OF MYTILENE
Like the hyacinth
there is a light
blinding my eyes.

220   A RETURN
Safe now. I've flown to you
like a child to its mother.

221   OUT OF ALL MANKIND
Is there in any land
any man whom you love
more than you love me?

222   I WOULD FLY TO THE VERY
FOOT OF YOUR MOUNTAINS
I would go anywhere
to take you in my arms
again, my darling.

223   TO HER DETRACTOR
As for him who blames me,
let him walk with madness
and stumble through sorrows.

224   A GIRL
One day I watched a tender girl
picking some wild flowers.

225   HOMECOMING
Soft girl from whom I was
altogether cut off,
I have come home again.

226 WEATHERCOCKS
Those whom I treated kindly
especially injure me now.

227 HAVING REFUSED TO ACCEPT
THE BITTER WITH THE SWEET
I will never find again
honey or the honey bees.

228 REST
The night closed their eyes
and then night poured down
black sleep upon their lids.

229 AN ENCOUNTER
You came to my house and sang to me,
and so I have come. Speak. Come down
and release me from the silence of
your beauty.

We were walking near your home when you
saw us. Now I ask: quickly, send your
girls away, and may the gods grant me
what they will.

230 TO A FRIEND
When I look at you, it is not
Hermione I think of: a mortal girl,
but I am moved as before the beauty
of blond Helen.

231 KLEÏS
I have a small daughter who is beautiful
like a gold flower. I would not trade
my darling Kleïs for all Lydia or even
for lovely Lesbos.

232 FROM HER EXILE

I have no embroidered headband
for you, Kleïs, and no idea
where to find one while Myrsilos

rules in Mytilene. The bright
ribbon reminds me of those days
when our enemies were in exile.

233 BETRAYAL

You have done wrong, Mika,
and I will not concur:
you have chosen to be friends
with the house of Penthilos.
Yet now we hear a sweet intrusion,
a voice like honey
from the loud-singing nightingale
in the dewy branches.

234 TO APHRODITE AND THE NEREIDS

Kyprian and Nereids, I beg you
to bring my brother home safely,
and let him accomplish whatever
is in his heart.

Let him amend his former errors
and be a joy to his friends but
a terror to enemies—though never
again to us.

Let him do honor to his sister,
and be free of the black torment
which in other days of sorrow
ravaged his soul.

235   AGAINST DORICHA, HER BROTHER'S
        MISTRESS

Kyprian, may she find you harsh
and find no occasion to brag: I
Doricha, got my love to come back
    a second time.

236   AGE AND LIGHT

Here are fine gifts, children,
O friend, singer on the clear tortoise lyre,

all my flesh is wrinkled with age,
my black hair has faded to white,

my legs can no longer carry me,
once nimble like a fawn's,

but what can I do?
It cannot be undone,

no more than can pink-armed Dawn
not end in darkness on earth,

or keep her love for Tithonos,
who must waste away;

yet I love refinement, and beauty and light
are for me the same as desire for the sun.

237   DREAM

O dream from the blackness,
come when I am sleeping.

Sweet is the god but still I am
in agony and far from my strength,

for I had hopes to share
something of the happy ones,

    [90]

nor was I so foolish
as to scorn pleasant toys.

Now may I have
all these things.

238   THE LAUREL TREE

You lay in wait
behind a laurel tree,

and everything
was pleasant:

you a woman
wanderer like me.

I barely heard you,
my darling;

you came in your
trim garments,

and suddenly: beauty
of your garments.

239   FOR PELAGON*

Pelagon the fisherman. His father
Meniskos placed here a fishbasket
and oar: relics of a wretched life.

240   EMPTINESS

I have never found you
so repulsive, O peace.†

* Probably not by Sappho.
† The word "peace" may be the name "Iranna."

[91]

241   A WOMAN'S PLEA
       I pray for long life and health.
       My children, I would escape
       from wrinkles and cling to youth.

242   SAPPHO SAYS*
       Death is our evil. The gods believe this,
       or else by now they would be dead.

243   ON TIMAS†
       Here is the dust of Timas who unmarried
       was led into Persephone's dark bedroom,
       and when she died her girlfriends took sharp
       iron knives and cut off their soft hair.

244   ACHILLES
       He lies now in the black earth,
       and the many sorrows are ended
       which he bore for the Atreidai.‡

245   ARTEMIS§
       To blond Apollo—child of Koios' daughter
       after she lay with our famous lord Zeus—
       Artemis swore an oath of the gods,
       swore by the beard of her father:
       "I shall always be a virgin
       and live on summits of the great sierras,
       hunting in the forests: O grant me this!"
       Her father nodded in approval. Now gods
       and mortals call her by her thrilling name:
       the deer-slaying hunter,
       and she is pure of marriage or erotic love.

* Probably not by Sappho.
† Probably not by Sappho.
‡ Probably Menelaos.
§ Attributed to Alkaios by Lobel and Page, to Sappho by Max Treu.

246   THE SWAN'S GIFT

It is said that Leda long ago
found a hidden egg the color
of hyacinths.

247   IT IS LATE

Even if you love me, find
a younger woman. I could
never bear to share my bed
with a man younger than I.

248   BITTERSWEET LOVE

It brings us pain
and weaves myths.

249   YOU FORGOT

And I am now wholly
gone into oblivion.

250   HER FRIENDS

No, my heart can never change
toward you who are so lovely.

251   EVENING STAR

Hesperos, you bring home all the bright dawn
     disperses,
bring home the sheep,
bring home the goat, bring the child home to its
     mother.*

* In Bruno Snell's reading the bright dawn brings *out* the sheep, goat
and the child away from its mother.

252   TO HERMES
Hermes came to me in a dream. I said
—My master, I am altogether lost,
and my many riches do not console me.
I care only
              to die, and watch the dewy lotus
along the banks of Acheron, river of Hell.

253   LAST PRAISES
If my nipples were to drip milk
and my womb still carry a child,
I would enter this marriage bed
                    intrepidly,

but age dries my flesh with a thousand
wrinkles, and love is in no hurry
to seize my body with the gifts
                    of pleasant pain.

Yet, let us sing praises to her
who wears the scent of violets
                    on her young breasts.

254   TO HER DAUGHTER
       WHEN SAPPHO WAS DYING
It would be wrong for us. It is not right
for mourning to enter a home of poetry.

255   HER WEALTH
The golden Muses gave me
true riches: when dead
I shall not be forgotten.

256   SOMEONE, I TELL YOU
Someone, I tell you,
will remember us.

We are oppressed by
fears of oblivion

yet are always saved
by judgment of good men.

257   HADES*
In all the dominions of the gods
only Death allows no place for sweet hope.

258   EROS
Now in my
heart I
see clearly

a beautiful
face
shining,

etched
by love.

259   SAPPHO, I LOVED YOU
Andromeda
forgot,

and I too
blamed you,

yet Sappho
I loved you.

In Kypros I am Queen
and to you a power

* This is also attributed to Alkaios.

as sun of fire
is a glory to all.

Even in Hades
I am with you.

260　DAWN
the queenly dawn.

Solon

A member of the Athenian aristocracy, Solon had begun his poetic activity earlier than ca. 600 B.C. For it was at this time that he wrote an elegy to his fellow citizens urging them to the reconquest of Salamis. But the most notable part of his life, and the subject of a good deal of his surviving poetry, was his involvement in the Athenian Social Question. In the conflict between the landed grandees and the dispossessed peasants (many of whom had been enslaved through debt) Solon took a middle position. In 594-593 B.C. he was elected as an Archon with extraordinary powers to carry out social and constitutional reforms in an effort to avoid civil war and revolution. Among other things, he abolished existing debts, established a council of four hundred as a counterweight to the aristocratic council of the Areiopagos and gave each class of the citizenry a certain voice in the political affairs of the country. After making his laws (and his name of course has since become a synonym for legislator), he bound the people to retain them unchanged for ten years, and went abroad for the duration. As one would expect, Solon displeased both sides by his moderation, and in fact the détente he had effected came to nothing in the end: Athens spent a good part of the sixth century under a tyranny based on the support of the commoners. However, even under the tyranny much of the substance of his reforms was retained, and the Solonian spirit, with its insight and discretion, prepared the way for the later brilliant and precarious forms of Athenian democracy.

The poetry of Solon, which constitutes the first Athenian literature, includes elegiac and iambic verse. The subject matter is political and moral, but also sometimes convivial and erotic.

It seems that the three most democratic aspects of Solon's rule were: first and greatest, the prohibition of loans on the person; second, the right of redress

for those who were wronged; third, the right of
appeal to courts of law, which more than all else
strengthened the people. Once master of the vote,
the people became master of the constitution.

ARISTOTLE, *Constitution of Athens*

He died in Kypros at the age of eighty. He left
orders with his family to have his bones taken to
Salamis and there burn them to ashes and scatter
them over the soil.

DIOGENES LAERTIOS, *Life of Solon*

And when Kroisos (Croesus) stood on the pyre, in
such an evil moment, it is said that he remembered
how truly inspired was Solon's saying that no mortal
is happy.

HERODOTOS, *Histories*

◇◇◇◇◇◇◇◇◇◇◇◇◇◇◇◇◇◇◇◇◇◇◇◇◇◇◇◇

261   APOLOGIA OF HIS RULE

Where did I fail? When did I give up goals
for which I gathered my torn people together?
When the judgment of time descends on me,
call on my prime witness, Black Earth, supreme
excellent mother of the Olympian gods,
whose expanse was once pocked with mortgage
        stones,
which I dug out to free a soil in bondage.

Into our home, Athens, founded by the gods,
I brought back many sold unlawfully as slaves,
and throngs of debtors harried into exile,
drifting about so long in foreign lands
they could no longer use our Attic tongue;
here at home men who wore the shameful brand
of slavery and suffered the hideous moods
of brutal masters—all these I freed. Fusing
justice and power into an iron weapon,
I forced through every measure I had pledged.
I wrote the laws for good and bad alike,
and gave an upright posture to our courts.

Had someone else controlled the whip of power,
a bungler, a man of greed, he would not
have held the people in. Had I agreed
to do what satisfied opponents, or else
what their enemies planned in turn for them,
our dear city would be widowed of her men.
But I put myself on guard at every side,
spinning like a wolf among a pack of dogs.

262   CIVIL WAR IN ATTICA
        I know it, and sorrow lives in my heart
        that the oldest land of Ionia is burning.

263   THE SIGNS OF DICTATORSHIP
        The power of hail and snow springs from a cloud,
            and thunder from the fire of lightning.
        Strong men destroy a city, and a tyrant
            enslaves a people through their ignorance.
        A ship once out of port is hard to capture:
            know this now before it is too late.

264   TO PHOKOS
        (On his refusal to assume dictatorial
        powers from which there is no retreat.)
        If I have spared my country
        by not descending into tyranny and unrelenting
            violence;
        if I have not piled odious dung on my good name,
        I am unashamed.
        No, I contend that my policy
        won far greater victories with common man.

265   INDIFFERENCE TO WEALTH
        Vast silver, gold, wheatlands, horses, mules
            are only equal to the wealth
        of him whose belly, ribs and feet are warm,
            who may be poor but enters love

with men or women when he comes upon
   the proper season in his youth.
This is plenitude for man. No one goes down
   to Hades with fabulous belongings.
Even ransom will not spare him from repugnant
   disease, evil old age and death.

266   VIRTUE AMONG THE POOR

    Many malicious men are rich. Many good men
       suffer through poverty. Yet who would trade
    virtue for gold? While the name of virtue endures
       money drops from hand to hand, lasting little.

267   SOLON BEFORE THE CROWDS IN ATHENS

    I am a herald from lovely Salamis. In place
       of talk I bring a song: an ornament of words.

268   A CITY OF TEN THOUSAND IN TEARS

    May I meet death without tears. But let my death
       bring sorrow and mourning to my friends.

269   LESSON IN CITIZENSHIP

    You must obey the law of the land,
    whether you think it right or wrong.

270   THE EROTIC MAN

    In the tender flower of youth he loves a boy,
       desiring his thighs and delicious mouth.

271   THE GODS

    The mind of the eternal gods
    can not be seen by man.

272 MORTAL MAN
No mortal is happy, and all men on earth
who look upon the sun are wretched.

273 TEN AGES IN THE LIFE OF MAN
A boy who is still a child grows baby teeth
and loses them all in seven years.
When God makes him fourteen, the signs of
maturity begin to shine on his body.
In the third seven, limbs growing, chin bearded,
his skin acquires the color of manhood.
In the fourth age a man is at a peak in
strength—a sign in man of excellence.
The time is ripe in the fifth for a young man
to think of marriage and of offspring.
In the sixth the mind of man is trained in all
things; he doesn't try the impossible.
In the seventh and eighth, that is, fourteen years,
he speaks most eloquently in his life.
He can still do much in the ninth but his speech
and thought are discernibly less keen;
and if he makes the full measure of ten sevens,
when death comes, it will not come too soon.

Mimnermos

*Mimnermos was active around 600 B.C. or some
ten years later. He was a citizen of either Kolophon
or Smyrna. The milieu of his poetry is that of the
Anatolian Greek city, fighting against Oriental
domination, but already under various sorts of
Oriental influence, including that of intermarriage.
Mimnermos' name is apparently itself Oriental. He
is symptom and spokesman of the decadence of
Ionia, enervated by despair and by pleasure.*

*His works included a Smyrneid (long poem on the
history of Smyrna) and a collection of elegies
probably addressed to Nanno (a flute-girl who
accompanied the performance of his poems) and
dealing in part with his love. In his erotic elegies
Mimnermos is one of the ancestors of the later love-
elegists of Alexandria and Rome.*

Mimnermos discovered the sweet sound and soft
breath of iambic pentameter, after much suffering.
He loved Nanno. . . . reveled with Examyes and
irritated the oppressive Hermobios and hostile
Pherekles because he hated their verse.

HERMESIANAX IN PHOTIOS, *Library*

If as Mimnermos says, there is not joy without love
and play, then you should live with love and play.

HORACE, *Epistles*

274   CENSURE OF AGE

What good is life when golden love is gone?
Frankly, I would rather be dead than ignore
a girl's warm surrender, her soft arms in bed
at night: lovely flower of youth that all women
and men desire!
                    When old age comes
a man feels feeble and ugly and crawls under
a crushing sorrow.

He loses the simple joy
of looking at the sun.
Children despise him.
He is repulsive to young women—in this sad
blind alley which God has made of old age.

275   TIME

When a man's good hour is past
though he once shone among mortals
he is neither honored nor loved.
Not even his own children favor him.

276   NOW

Be young, dear soul. Soon others will be men
   and I being dead will be black earth.

277   A PLEDGE

Between us, dear friend,
let there always be truth,
most just of all things.

278   FOR THE GOLDEN FLEECE

Jason went to the city of King Aietes
where the sun's swift rays are stored
in a gold chamber by the ocean's lips.

279   REFUGE AGAINST TALK

Be happy in your own soul. Among pitiless
   townsmen
   one will always abuse you, another speak praise.

280   A WARRIOR OF THE LYDIAN WARS

No man could match his strength or heroic heart,
   so the elders told me who had seen him

cutting through the phalanx of massed Lydian
    cavalry,
  swinging his ashwood spear on the plain
of Hermos. Pallas Athene could find no fault
    with the stinging courage in his heart
when he plunged first-line into the bloody clash,
    rushing through the rain of bitter shafts.
No man ever battled more bravely than he
    when he darted forward like a ray of sun.

281   HELIOS AT NIGHT

The sun works every day and there's no rest
    for him or for his horses once
the rose-fingered dawn leaves the ocean waters
    and begins to scale the firmament.
For with night the sun is swept across the waves
    in a hollow cup of gleaming gold,
a wondrous bed with wings, forged by Hephaistos;
    it speeds him sleeping over salt foam
from the Hesperides to the Ethiopian desert.
    There his fleet chariot and horses wait
till Dawn comes, early child of morning.

282   EXPECTATION

Like fragile shoots in the polyflowered spring
    growing quickly in amazing sun,
we love the blossom of youth for a brief season
    knowing from the gods nothing of evil
or good. Yet near us loom black Keres, and
    painful old age, or worse, death.
The fruit-tree of our life ripens swiftly like
    a morning sun. But our brilliance gone,
we are soon better dead than alive. Our heart
    is torn, our home is dark with poverty.
One man longs for a son and goes down childless
    into Hell; another shrivels in murderous
disease. No man on earth eludes the net
    of unending sorrows sent by Zeus.

283 EXPEDITION

We left the craggy city of Neleian Pylos
and came on ship to handsome Asia
and lovely Kolophon our base.
There we brashly mustered our immense army
    in dreadful pride,
and set out along the river flowing inside
    the forest.
Aided by the gods
we captured the Aiolian city of Smyrna.

Phokylides

*Perhaps a contemporary of Solon and Mimnermos
(ca. 600 B.C.), Phokylides was a citizen of Miletos.
He wrote a series of maxims, each with the "seal"
of the author (i.e., each beginning with a formula
which included the author's name). Some have seen
in this pride of authorship a sign of the new
consciousness of the individual. Phokylides wrote in
dactylic hexameters instead of elegiacs. (The verses
known as the* Carmen Phokylideum *are an
interesting 230-line succession of maxims written
by either a Jew or a Christian ca.* A.D. 100.)

To prove this we might consider the poetry of
Hesiod, Theognis and Phokylides, who are declared
to be the best counselors ever known in matters
of human life.

ISOKRATES, *To Nikokles*

Archilochos may be reproached for his subject
matter, Parmenides for his prosody and Phokylides
for his poverty of expression. . . . Yet each deserves
praise for his special innate ability to stir and lead
his audience.

PLUTARCH, *On Listening*

284   APPEARANCE OF WISDOM
Many empty-headed clods pass by like sages
when they walk with chin erect and stern eyes.

285   ON THE PROBLEM OF CHOOSING A WIFE
In the words of Phokylides: the tribes of women
come in four breeds: bee, bitch and grimy sow,
and sinewy mare with draping mane. The mare
is healthy, swift, roundly built and on the loose.

[106]

The monster-looking sow is neither good nor
      rotten,
and the bristling bitch lies snapping at the leash.

Yes, the bee is best: a whizz at cleaning, trim
and good in cooking. My poor friend, I tell you,
for a bright, balmy marriage, pray for a bee.

Asios

Of Samos. Sixth century B.C. *Wrote genealogies,
satirical hexameters, elegiacs, etc.*

In the epic poems of Asios, son of Amphiptolemos
of Samos, Phoinix had two daughters by Perimede,
daughter of Oineos. These were Astypalaia and
Europa.

PAUSANIAS, *Description of Greece*

You are blind to history, Sir Potbelly. You are an
ass-licker, and to recall the old Samian poet Asios,
an ass-kisser.

ATHENAIOS, *Doctors at Dinner*

286   AN OLD PARASITE
Clubfoot, branded like a runaway slave,
the old ass-kisser came like a beggar,
crashing the wedding party of Meles.
He asked for soup and stood among us
like a phantom risen from the mud.

Stesichoros

A poet who was ranked with Homer by some of the ancients, Stesichoros was born in Sicily around 630 B.C. and died around 555 B.C. He was active both at Akragas (where he seems to have come into conflict with the tyrant Phalaris) and Himera. He may have made a visit to mainland Greece, and Sparta in particular.

His works were abundant: they were arranged in twenty-six books by the Alexandrian scholars. They seem to have involved a confluence of the Doric choral traditions and the Ionian epic, with an admixture of local Sicilian legend. Stesichoros introduced full-fledged narrative into choral poetry, and told his stories more directly than, e.g., Pindar. Among the subjects of his narratives were Herakles, Europa, Helen, the Sack of Troy and the Orestes legend. Tradition further ascribes to Stesichoros the innovation of the triadic structure of the choral ode (strophe, antistrophe and epode). His language was Doric, with strong Homeric influence.

The influence of Stesichoros on the subjects of sixth-century painting was apparently very great. Thanks to Stesichoros, Athena was shown fully armed at birth, Herakles acquired his club, lionskin and bow, and Geryon his wings. If more of him had survived, the effect on the literature of modern Europe would probably have been greater than if Alkman, Ibykos or even Simonides had been preserved entire.

There is a story that while Sokrates was in prison, awaiting his death, he heard a man sing skillfully a song by the lyric poet Stesichoros, and begged him to teach it to him before it was too late, and when the musician asked why, Sokrates replied, "I want to die knowing one thing more."

AMMIANUS MARCELLINUS

<><><><><><><><><><><><><><><><><><><><><><><><>

287   ON THE ILIAD
        The white-horsed myth.

288   RECANTATION TO HELEN*
        I spoke nonsense and I begin again:

        The story is not true.
        You never sailed on a benched ship.
        You never entered the city of Troy.

289   ON KLYTAIMNESTRA

                                    Foreseeing the end of
                                    the Aigisthos line.
        She dreamed that a serpent appeared
                            with blood-dripping scales,
        and from his belly stepped a king
                            from the ancient dynasty
        of Pleisthenes and Agamemnon.

290   ON THE MARRIAGE
        OF HELEN AND MENELAOS
        Many quince apples were cast upon the chariot
           of the king,
        many leaves of myrtle,
        hundreds of roses and thousands of braided violets.

291   ON THE MARRIAGE OF ADMETOS
        AND ALKESTIS
                        Bring your virgin's dowry
        cakes of every kind—sesame, groats, sweet oil—
                    and bring yellow honey too.

---

* According to Plato in the *Phaedros*, when Stesichoros was blinded for
having slandered Helen, he, unlike Homer who was blinded for the same
sin, wrote a *Palinode*, a recantation, and immediately recovered his sight.

292   BIRTHPLACE OF EURYTION
Eurytion was born in famous Erytheia
in the hollow of a rock,
near the inexhaustible silver-rooted springs
      of the river in Tartessos.

293   HERAKLES' QUEST OF THE CATTLE OF
GERYON
Then the sungod Helios, child of Hyperion,
soared in his gold-flashing bowl above the ocean
and entered the depths of black holy night,
seeking his mother, young wife and darling
      children.

But crossing the land on foot was Herakles, son of
      Zeus,
on his mission through the shadowy laurel grove.

294   A KING'S PUNISHMENT
On the day of sacrifice,
Tyndareos remembered all the gods but one:
      the gift-giving Kyprian,
and in her rage the queen of love
made his daughters marry two times
and three times,
made them walk out on their husbands.

295   ON SONG AND LAMENT
Apollo loves happy play and cadenced singing
but he leaves groans and mourning to Hades.

Yet how futile even to weep for the dead—
for when dead, a man's glory dies among men.

296   SEASON OF SONG
        Forget the wars.
        It is time to sing.
        Take out the flute from Phrygia
        and recall the songs of our blond Graces.

        Clamor of babbling swallows:
        it is already spring.

Ibykos

*Born of a noble family at Rhegium in the toe of
Italy in the first half of the sixth century B.C.,
Ibykos went to the island of Samos after he had
begun his poetic career. It is said that he went to
Samos as an alternative to assuming the tyranny
which was offered him in his native town. In any
case, he went probably at the invitation of the
famous Tyrant of Samos, Polykrates, who made his
court a center of culture and sophistication—
Anakreon was another of Polykrates' guests. Ibykos
was said to have been murdered by robbers and
avenged by birds who were present at the murder.
(See Schiller's ballad "The Cranes of Ibykos.")*

*In his work, Ibykos brought about a fusion of the
West Greek choral lyric as developed by Stesichoros
and the East Greek personalism as seen, e.g., in
Alkaios and Sappho. In his early work Ibykos seems
clearly to have followed Stesichoros' tradition of
lyric narrative ("On Herakles" is probably a
fragment from this period). But on moving to
Samos, he appropriated erotic themes to the choral
form, giving them a more ornate and elaborate
expression than they had received at the hands of
the monodists. Both subject and style, it may be
imagined, suited the tastes of the Polykratean
court. His language is the composite language of
most choral poetry, with Doric traces.*

Caught by robbers in a deserted spot, he was killed
exclaiming that the very cranes which flew over at
the moment would be his avengers. Some time
afterward one of the robbers saw some cranes in the
city and cried, "Look! the avengers of Ibykos."
Whereupon one of the bystanders enquired into the
matter of this speech of his. The crime was admitted,
and the robbers brought to justice. Hence the
proverb: "The cranes of Ibykos."

The *Suda Lexicon*

As foolish as Ibykos.

PROVERB BY DIOGENES

What extravagant things Alkaios writes on the love
of youths! And as for Anakreon, his poetry is erotic
from beginning to end. Yet to judge from his works
they all were surpassed in this matter by Ibykos of
Rhegium. And the love of all these poets was
sensual love.

CICERO

297   LOVE'S SEASON

In spring the quince trees
ripen in the girls' holy orchard
with river waters;
and grapes turn violet
under the shade of luxuriant leafage
and newborn shoots.

But for me, Eros
knows no winter sleep, and as north winds
burn down from Thrace
with searing lightning,
Kypris mutilates my heart with black
and baleful love.

298   MORNING

Dawn that ends our sleep
also wakes
the loud nightingale.

299   LIKE AN OLD CHAMPION

Even now Eros looks at me with tenderness
from under dark eyelids, and casts me spellbound
into Aphrodite's nets where I lie caught
inextricably,

for I swear his mere approach makes me tremble
like an old champion chariot horse, as he
draws a swift cart unwillingly to the race.

[114]

300   RESEMBLING THE BIRDS

In the high branches perch the mottled ducks
and purple cormorants with their sleek throats
and kingfishers of the long wings.

O let my heart always be like the birds
of the purple crest and long wings!

301   ON FLOWERS

Myrtles and violets and yellow cassidonies,
apple flowers and roses and glossy laurel.

302   ON EURYALOS

Euryalos, child of the exquisite Graces
and darling of the lovely-haired Muses,
you were reared by Kypris and soft-eyed Peitho
among the blossoms of the rose.

303   ON FEMININE NATURE
AND PUBLIC DECENCY

                    Spartan girls
are naked-thighed and man-crazy.

304   CONSTELLATION

Burning across the endless night
like brilliant Dog Stars.

305   ON HERAKLES

I killed the boys on the white horse,
the sons of Molione.

Their bodies were alike; their age
and faces were identical—being
twins and born together
in a silver egg.

306   THE IMPOSSIBLE
When a man is dead one can find
no medicine to bring him life.

307   ON A MAN-MADE PENINSULA
IN SYRACUSE
With mortal hands they joined the island
of Ortygia to the stony mainland,
where once there was a hunting zone
for seasnails and carnivorous fish.

Hipponax

Hipponax was banished from Ephesos ca. 545 B.C.
He spent much time as a wandering beggar in the
neighboring city of Klazomenai. He seems to have
had quarrels with two sculptors named Boupalos and
Athenis. There are indications of a liaison with the
former's girlfriend Arete.

In style and subject matter Hipponax is set off
from the other major poets of the Lyric Age by his
total preoccupation with private topics and his
adoption of the demotic manner. He is for Adrados
an instance of the increasing dissolution of
*Hellenism in the Greek cities of Asia Minor.**

Hipponax wrote choliambs ("lame" iambics, also
known as "scazons," with a dragging final foot in
each line), other iambic and trochaic verse,
hexameters and epodes—not the epodes of a choral
triad, but, as with Archilochos, a quasi-stanzaic form
usually composed of two different kinds of metrical
lines.

Hipponax influenced Greek comedy, and was the
fountainhead of several different types of choliambic
poetry: Kallimachos' iambics, Herondas, Kerkidas,
etc.

O stranger, stay clear of the horrible tomb of
Hipponax, which hurls abuse as thick as hail and
whose very ashes compose iambics in hatred of
Boupalos. You might wake the sleeping wasp
whose bile would not rest even in Hades, but
launches straight shafts of song in lame measure.†

PHILIPPOS, *Palatine Anthology*

---

* Adrados, *Líricos griegos*, II, 13.
† Hipponax invented the choliamb, or lame iambic.

308   ON THE SCOUNDREL BOUPALOS
      Hold my coat while I belt Boupalos in the eye.
      I am ambidextrous and never miss a punch.

309   KEEP GOING, MONSTER*
      Keep going, monster, all the long way to Smyrna.
      Pass through Lydia and past the tomb of Attales,
      the grave of King Gyges and the stele of
          Megastrys,
      the funereal monument of Atys, and king of
          Attalyda,
      and turn your belly toward the sinking sun.

310   MIDWIFE
      What navel-snipper wiped you, god-blasted one,
      and washed you as you kicked about the floor?

311   ON A SERPENT PAINTED AT
      THE WRONG END OF A SHIP
      Mimnes, you degenerate artist! Don't paint
      a snake running up the rear end
      of our trireme.†
      Unbearable disgrace and evil luck
      will tag us, slave of slaves. You leave the
          helmsman
      open to being bitten on the shins.

312   PRAYER TO HERMES
      Hermes, dear Hermes, Maia's son from Kyllene,
      I pray to you, for I'm frozen and I shiver.

   * Attales: Brother of Alyattes, King of Persia, whose tomb still exists.
Megastrys: Lover of Gyges. Atys: mythical lover of Kybeles. Attalyda:
founder of city of same name. Text is corrupt and with many variations
and interpretations.
   † A galley having three banks of oars.

Give Hipponax a woolen overcoat, a Persian
cape, some sandals and felt slippers,
and sixty gold staters for his inner wall.

Give Hipponax a woolen overcoat. I tell you,
his teeth are rattling in his head!

But from you never even a shabby coat against
    the very cold
or slippers to keep my toes from freezing.

313   WAYS OF PROVIDENCE
       Never yet has the blind god, Wealth,
       come to my house and said: "Hipponax,
       I'm giving you thirty silver minas
       and much more." No, he's far too tight.

314   A NEW CHARYBDIS
       O Muse, sing to me of that sea-monster,
           Eurymedon's son,*
       whose stomach, like a knife, fattens on all it finds.
       Tell of his dreadful end, and how by public order
       the town will stone him to death beside the sterile
           sea.

315   MEDICATION FOR SADNESS
       I will abandon my agonized soul to vice
       if instantly you don't send a medimnos
       of barley. From the flour I'll make a brew
       to drink as medicine against my sorrows.

316   MISERIES
       In a Lydian voice she said, "Come quick,
       I will plug up your tight asshole."
       And she beat my balls with a branch

* Parody of Homer.

[119]

as though I were a scapegoat. I tripped,
and stuck on the gallows I suffered
a double torture: a branch lashed
my chest; someone wet me with cowshit
and my ass stank. Beetles came, drawn
by the stinking gook like summer flies.
They fell on me, shoved, filing their teeth
on my bones. The invasion complete,
I ached more than from a Pygelian plague.

317   INJUSTICE
It is outrageous. Now they rail at Kritias,
    the upright islander from Chios,
and condemn him for adultery,
merely because they saw him
wandering in the rooms of a cathouse.

Anakreon

The only great Ionian monodist was born in Teos
in Asia Minor around 572 B.C. Soon after the
capture of Sardis by the Persians in 541 B.C.
Anakreon fled with his fellow townsmen to Abdera
in Thrace, and established a colony there. "On a
Virgin" may date from this period. The Tyrant of
Samos, Polykrates, invited him to come and teach
his son music and poetry. Anakreon and Ibykos thus
both were poetic luminaries of the court of Samos.
Anakreon in particular seems temperamentally
suited to the sophisticated conviviality and
eroticism which was the Polykratean style. In 522 B.C.
Polykrates was killed by Persian treachery, and
Anakreon went to Athens—in a boat, it is said, sent
especially for him by Hipparchos, brother of the
reigning Athenian tyrant Hippias. Hipparchos, who
was a sort of cultural commissar under his brother,
seems to have fostered a style of life much like that
at Samos under Polykrates. Upon the assassination
of Hipparchos in 514 B.C. Anakreon moved to
Thessaly for a time, but was then received back in
Athens (now a democracy) with apparently no hard
feelings over his earlier friendship with the tyrants.
During this period he was a friend of Xanthippos,
the father of Perikles. Anakreon died at the age of
eighty-five, probably soon after 490 B.C. The legend
was that he choked, appropriately, on a grape pip.

The works of Anakreon, in six books, consisted of
lyrics (mainly monodic), iambics and elegiacs. The
bulk of the surviving fragments are lyric. The
language of Anakreon is almost entirely the Ionian
of his day.

The most remarkable feature of the poetry of
Anakreon, the one most commented on, is its
varying tone of playfulness, sophistication,
detachment or irony (as seen, for instance, in "The
Vision of Love," "On an Old Lover" and
"Preparations for Love").

His influence in later poetry has probably been
greater than that of either Alkaios or Sappho. The

numerous two-dimensional projections in the
Anakreonteia *are often delightful, but sweet, not*
savory. Horace adapted some themes. But the poetry
of Renaissance France and England is the locus of
the most flourishing Anakreonism. Even though
filtered in large part through the Anakreonteia, *the*
poet's manner is still perceptible in Ronsard, Herrick,
Ben Jonson and others.

Anakreon's poetic works are entirely erotic.
CICERO, *Tusculan Disputations*

The grammarian Didymos wrote four thousand
books . . . in which he discusses whether Anakreon
was more of a rake than a sot, whether Sappho was
a prostitute, and other questions the answers to
which you should forget if you knew them.
SENECA, *Letters to Lucilius*

Stranger, passing near the tomb of Anakreon,
pour me a libation as you approach,
for in life I was a drunkard.
ANONYMOUS

318   ARTEMIS
On my knees I speak to you,
Artemis, hunter of deer,
blond child of Zeus and queen
of roaming beasts. From pools
of the river Lethaios you gaze
across a city of brave men.
Serenity. You are a shepherd
of no flock of savage citizens.

319   DICE
The dice of love are
shouting and madness.

320   THE VISION OF LOVE

On easy wings I glide to Olympos where
I seek my master Eros,
but he no longer lets me run down warm women
as in my doghood days:
he sees my graying beard and passes me by,
while I stand transfixed
in the wind made by his wings of quivering gold.

321   ON AN OLD LOVER

Eros, the blond god of lovers,
strikes me with a purple ball
and asks me to play with a girl
    wearing colorful sandals;

but the girl is from beautiful
Lesbos, and scorns my white hair,
and turning her back runs gaping
    behind another girl.

322   ON A VIRGIN

My Thracian foal, why do you glare with disdain
and then shun me absolutely as if I knew
    nothing of this art?

I tell you I could bridle you with tight straps,
seize the reins and gallop you around the posts
    of the pleasant course.

But you prefer to graze on the calm meadow,
or frisk and gambol gayly—having no manly
    rider to break you in.

323   PREPARATIONS FOR LOVE

Bring out water and wine and an armful
of flowers.
I want the proper setting
when I spar a few rounds with love.

324   KNOCKOUT

Eros, the blacksmith of love,
smashed me with a giant hammer
and doused me in the cold river.

325   THE PLUNGE

Lord! I clamber up the white cliff
and dive into the steaming wave,
            O dead drunk with love.

326   ON A CONSERVATIVE LOVER

I love and yet do not love.
I am mad yet not quite mad.

327   DEFINITION OF A WHORE

Given-to-all and
            celebrated by the masses,
a carrier-of-peoples
              and an apple orchard
        of mad haunches.

328   ON STREETWALKERS

Although we call these women loose,
they tighten their thighs around thighs.

329   ON THE FORTUNES OF ARTEMON

Once he went about in filthy clothes and waspy
    hair,
with wooden rings on his ears, and wore around
    his ribs
an unwashed hairy oxhide from an old miserable
    shield.
Our con-man pimped a living from bakery girls
    and whores,

and got his neck bound to a whipping block where
    the leather
made raw meat of his back—and best, he rode the
    wheel
so that hairs could be torn from his beard and
    scalp.

But now the good Artemon rides like a generous
    lord
in an excellent coach or litter; he wears gold
    earrings
and carries a special ivory parasol like a grand
    lady.

330   CHARIOTEER

    O sweet boy like a girl,
    I see you though you will not look my way.
    You are unaware that you handle the reins
        of my soul.

331   ON DRINKING PARTIES*

    I do not like the man who sits by his bowl
        and sobs about the sad wars,
    but the rake who loves to rave about fine feats
        in the arts and art of love.

332   A WAY TO THE HEART

                Come swiftly
    and rub aromatic myrrh on her breasts:
    the hollow cave around her heart.

333   ON THE ORIGIN OF MULES OR HALF-ASSES

    The Mysians were first in perfecting the art
    of coupling mare-hopping donkeys with horses.

* Attributed to Semonides by Bergk.

334   OF EFFEMINACY
In the morning they were joined in marriage,
though later in the same chamber
the groom could not join with his wife.

335   DECEMBER
We go through Poseidon's month.
Ponderous clouds sag with water
and furious storms break out
collapsing the rain earthward.

336   ON A HOPLITE
Here, the tomb of Timokritos, a hero in the wars.
It is the coward whom Ares spares—not the brave.

337   ON A GUARDIAN ANGEL
Now I hang in Athene's gleaming temple.
It was I who brought Python safely home
                        from the dreadful wars:
I, his shield.

338   VACILLATION
The bird flashes back and forth
between the black leaves of laurel trees
and the greenness of the olive grove.

339   ON THE SOLDIER AGATHON
All members of this village have come to weep
at your funeral pyre, O courageous Agathon,
who died for Abdera:

for in the chaos of the horrible battlefield,
blood-loving Ares never before slaughtered
a more fearless youth.

340   ON KLEINORIDES, LOST AT SEA*

You too, Kleinorides, were lost loving your country
as you confronted the wintry blast of the south
wind.
In the spring season of your life you died unwed;
the seawaves washed away your graceful adoles-
cence.

341   ENCOUNTER

I looked at her and took off
like a frightened cuckoo bird.

342   CANDOR

                    Personally,
I hate those who are furtive and touchy, morose
in their ways. I have learned that you, Megistes,
are of the innocent; of the childlike ones.

343   ON DEATH

My temples are white, my head largely bald.
Graceful youth has departed from my face,
and my teeth are loose teeth of an old man.
              I have few years left of sweet life.

Therefore I tremble and fear the underworld,
for the lightless chasm of death is dreadful
and the descent appalling: once cast down
              into Hell, there is no return.

344   PREPARATION

Let us hang garlands of celery
                 across our foreheads,
and call a festival to Dionysos.

* Also ascribed to Leonidas of Tarentum.

Xenophanes

Born in 565 B.C. in Kolophon (near Ephesos in Asia Minor), Xenophanes fled from the Persian invaders and settled in Elea, in Italy. He died sometime after 473 B.C. He seems to have been partly a philosopher and partly a rhapsode (professional reciter of poems), but the integration of the two roles is not a matter of common agreement. On the philosophical side Xenophanes is remarkable for his vigorous criticism of traditional myth and anthropomorphic religion, and for his espousal of a kind of pantheism. His works included "Silloi" (satiric and parodic hexameters), a poem "On Nature" and elegies. He wrote also two verse histories—of Elea and of Kolophon.

When someone related to Xenophanes that he had seen eels alive in hot water, he said: "Then we can boil them in cold."

PLUTARCH, *Common Notions against the Stoics*

Consider Xenophanes' remark that it is just as impious to say that the gods were born as to say that they died. Both statements imply that at some time they did not exist.

ARISTOTLE, *Rhetoric*

You Xenophaneses, Diagorases, Hippons, Epikouroses, and the rest of that catalogue of odious god-forsaken wretches, go drop dead.

AELIANUS

Xenophanes says there are four elements in existing things, and an infinite number of separate worlds. Clouds are made from vapor of the sun carried upward into the air. The essence of god is spherical, in no way resembling man. He is all

[128]

eyes and all ears but does not
breathe. He is in his totality mind
and thinking, and is eternal. Xenophanes
was the first to have declared
that all that exists is transitory and
destructible, and that the soul is
breath or spirit.

DIOGENES LAERTIOS, *Lives of the
Philosophers*

◇◇◇◇◇◇◇◇◇◇◇◇◇◇◇◇◇◇◇◇◇◇◇◇◇◇◇◇◇◇◇

345   BANQUET DECORUM

Now the floor is scrubbed clean, our hands are
    washed
    and cups are dry. A boy loops garlands
in our hair. Another passes round a phial
    of redolent balsam. The mixing bowl
is bubbling with good cheer, and more fragrant
    wine
    stands potent in the earthen jars.
Incense floats a holy perfume through the room.
    Water is cold, crystal, sweet.
Golden bread is set near on a princely table
    loaded down with cheese and rich honey.
The altar in the center is submerged in flowers
    and the house vibrates with fun and singing.

Gracious men should first sing praises to God
    with proper stories and pure words.
After the libation when we pray for strength
    to act with rectitude (our first concern),
there is no sin in drinking all one can
    and still get home without a servant—
unless too old. We commend the man who shows
    good memory after drink; who seeks virtue
and not to harangue us with the ancient myths
    of noisy wars of Titans, Giants,
Centaurs. These things are worth nothing. The
    good
    lies in our reverence for the gods.

346 GAY DAYS IN ASIATIC KOLOPHON
They acquired useless luxuries out of Lydia
    while still free from her odious tyranny;
paraded to the market place in seapurple robes,
    often in bright swarms of a thousand.
They were proud and pleased in their elaborate
    hairdo's
    and hid body odor with rare perfumes.

347 THE NATURE OF GOD
There is one God—supreme among gods and
    men—
who is like mortals in neither body nor mind.

348 AGNOSTIC CREDO
The truth is that no man ever was or will be
who understands the gods and all I speak of.
If you stumble on some rocks of the whole truth
you never know it. There is always speculation.

349 PYTHAGORAS AND THE TRANSMIGRATED
SOUL
One day a dog was being thrashed in the street,
and behold, Pythagoras, philosopher of spirits,
    was walking by.
                    His heart was in his mouth
for the poor pup.
                "Stop! Stop!" he cried.
"Don't beat him any more.
This is my dear friend's soul.
I recognize the voice when I hear him bark."

350 KNOWLEDGE
The gods did not enrich man
with a knowledge of all things
from the beginning of life.
Yet man seeks, and in time
invents what may be better.

[130]

351   THE MAKING OF GODS

1

Man made his gods, and furnished them
with his own body, voice and garments.

2

If a horse or lion or a slow ox
had agile hands for paint and sculpture,
the horse would make his god a horse,
the ox would sculpt an ox.

3

Our gods have flat noses and black skins
say the Ethiopians. The Thracians say
our gods have red hair and hazel eyes.

352   ON WATERS AND WINDS

Sea is a source of water and source of wind.
With no great ocean there would be no wind,
no moving rivers nor rainwater from the sky.
Great ocean is father of clouds, winds, rivers.

353   THE PHYSICAL ORIGIN OF THE RAINBOW

Whom they call Iris—is also a raincloud
which we see as purple, scarlet and green.

354   THE NATURE OF THE UNIVERSE

Everything comes from the earth,
and everything ends in the earth.

355   FIRST PRINCIPLES

All that is born and grows
comes from water and earth.

356   LAMPOON AGAINST HOMER AND HESIOD
       Homer and Hesiod emblazoned the gods
       with all that is shameful and scandalous
       in man:
       stealing, adultery and mutual deceit.

357   THE SHAPE OF THE EARTH
       At our feet we see this end of the earth
       where it rises to meet the firmament.
       Below, the world sinks down unendingly.

Simonides

*Pindar's stylistic antipode and sometime rival
was born of good family on the island of Keos
in 556 B.C. Like Anakreon he was one of the poets
invited to Athens by Hipparchos as part of the
program of cultural enrichment inaugurated under
the Peisistratid tyranny. It was probably at Athens
that he wrote the dithyrambs to which only one
brief reference survives. After the fall of the
tyranny—again like Anakreon—he went to
Thessaly under the patronage of several leading
houses. But he was back in Athens by 490, since
he is reported to have defeated the dramatist
Aischylos in a competition to write an epitaph
for those fallen at Marathon. During the period
of the Persian Wars he became as it were the poetic
spokesman for the whole of Greece, as his ode
on the fallen at Thermopylai would suggest. At
Athens he became the friend of Themistokles. In
476 B.C. at the age of eighty he went to Sicily,
where he was welcomed both at Syracuse and
Akragas. (Pindar was in Sicily at this same time.)
Simonides died in Sicily in 468/7 B.C. and was
buried at Akragas. The tradition reports that he
was ugly, and shrewd in money matters.*

*Simonides composed choral poetry in many
genres, especially threnoi and epinikia. He also
wrote elegies and elegiac epigrams. His dialect was
a mollified Doric in choral lyric, and in elegy—
as usual for this genre—predominantly Homeric.
In contrast to Pindar, his style in choral poetry
was on the whole direct and harmonious. His
epinikia seem, unlike those of Pindar, to have
been sportive and lighthearted. In outlook—
political, ethical, religious—he was more "modern"
and more adaptable by far than Pindar.*

"Still," I said, "I do not find it easy
to disbelieve a wise and inspired
artist like Simonides."

PLATO, Republic

[133]

When Simonides was discussing wisdom and riches with Hieron's wife,
and she asked him which was better, to
become wise or to become wealthy, he
replied, "To become wealthy. For I
see the wise sitting on the door-
steps of the rich."

ARISTOTLE, Rhetoric

His chief excellence lies in his pathos.
Indeed some consider that in this
quality he surpasses all other
writers in this kind of literature.

QUINTILIAN, Guide to Oratory

358 MEN OF THE FRONT RANKS

Through their extraordinary courage, the wide
farmlands of Tegea
have not shot fire and smoke into the sky.
For they made their choice
to leave their children in a country green
and sweet with freedom,
and died for this in the wild ranks of battle.

359 ON THE LAKEDAIMONIANS
FALLEN AT PLATAIA

These men left an altar of glory on their land,
shining in all weather,
when they were enveloped by the black mists of
   death.
but although they died
they are not dead, for their courage raises them in
   glory
from the rooms of Hell.

360   ON THE GREEKS FALLEN AT EURYMEDON

With mindless bravura Ares washed his long sleek
arrowheads
in the crimson waters within their chests,
and dust now lies not on the living flesh
of javelineers,
but on the vivid remnants of lifeless bodies.

361   ON THOSE WHO DIED AT THERMOPYLAI

Through their extraordinary courage, the wide
farmlands of Tegea
Their tomb is an altar on which stand our bowls
    of remembrance
and the wine of our praise.
Neither mold and worms, nor time
which destroys all things, will blacken their deaths.
The shrine of these brave men
has found its guardian
in the glory of Greece. Leonidas, the Spartan king,
lives in the great ornament he left behind
of unending fame and virtue.

362   GRAVE BY THE WATER

We were slaughtered in a Dirphian gully, and our
        graves,
    near Euripos, were paid for by our nation.
Justice. For in confronting the cruel clouds of war,
    we gave away our years of lovely youth.

363   ARETE*

Virtue lives on a high rock
painful to climb and guarded by
a band of pure and evasive nymphs.
No mortal may look upon her
unless sweat pours from his body
and he climbs the summit of manliness.

* Arete: virtue, courage, achievement.

364   INSCRIPTION FOR ATHENIAN HEROES
       WHO FOUGHT AT THE ISTHMOS
       When her fate rested on the razor's edge,
       we gave away our lives to save all Greece.

365   CODE OF HONOR AT THERMOPYLAI
       Stranger, go back to Sparta and tell our people
           that we who were slain obeyed the code.

366   VICTORY AT MARATHON
       At Marathon the Athenians fought for all Greece
       and broke the spearhead of Persia's crack troops.

367   ON THOSE WHO DIED WITH LEONIDAS
       Leonidas, king of the open fields of Sparta,
           those slain with you lie famous in their graves,
       for they attacked absorbing the head-on assault
           of endless Persian men, arrows and swift horse.

368   AN ORACLE'S DEATH AT THERMOPYLAI
       This is the tomb of famous Megistias, slain by
           the Persians near the Spercheios River,
       a seer who even when aware that death was near
           would not desert his Spartan kings.

369   ON MEGAKLES
       When I look at the tomb of Megakles
       with its dead body,
       I pity you, poor Kallia, his father.

370   CROSSING THE GULF OF CORINTH
       All these victors from the Tyrrhenian wars
       were on their way to Apollo at Delphi
       with their first plunder

       [136]

when they found their grave
on one night, in one ship, in one deep sea.

371 THE ATHENIAN VANGUARD

Athenian sons demolished the Persian army
and saved their country from painful slavery.

372 SOCIAL DICTUM

The city is the teacher of the man.

373 ON IPHIMENES

O Geraneia, tall-air mountain of evil,
I wish you faced the far Danube or Tanais,
river of distant Skythia;
that the Skeironian precipice did not rise
from the sea where Iphimenes sailed around
the broken rock of Molouris.
Now he is a frozen corpse in the gulf,
and this open tomb tells of his bitter voyage.

374 DANAË AND THE INFANT PERSEUS
     IMPRISONED IN A CHEST ON THE SEA

A tilting sea and thundering winds
tossed the carved chest and filled Danaë
with terror; she cried
and placed her arm lovingly around
Perseus saying: "My child, I suffer
and yet your heart is calm; you sleep
profoundly in the blue dark of night
and shine in our gloomy bronze-ribbed boat.
Don't think of the heaving saltwave
that seeps in through airholes and drenches
your hair, nor of the clamoring gale;
but lying in our seaviolet blanket
keep your lovely body close to mine.

[137]

If you knew the horror of our plight,
your gentle ears would hear my words.
But sleep, my son, and let
the ocean sleep and our great troubles end.
I ask you, father Zeus,
rescue us from our fate; and should
my words seem too severe, I beg you please
remember where we are, and forgive
my prayer."

375   ON LYKAS, A THESSALIAN HOUND

Bitch-hound, hunter, even your dead white bones
terrify the beasts of the field,
for your bravery is common knowledge
from huge Pelion to far Ossa
and on the dizzying sheep-paths of Kithairon.

376   HALCYON DAYS*

During the winter solstice
Zeus orders fourteen days of peaceful weather,
and man has called this windless season holy
for then the mottled halcyon rears its young.

377   ON A STATUE OF PHILON

I am from the island of Corfu.
My name: Philon, son of Glaukos.
And I am here,
because down in Olympia, at the games,
I was champion in boxing two years running.

378   VICTORY SONG FOR THE BOXER
       GLAUKOS OF KARYSTOS

Neither the knockout king Polydeukes
nor even Herakles (iron boy of Alkmena)
would put up his guard to the mighty Glaukos.

---

* "The halcyon nests about the time of the winter solstice, and that is
why, when the weather is fine at that time of year, we call the days
'Halcyon days.' " Aristotle, *History of Animals.*

379   A MODEST GRAVE
        Sir, you are not looking at the tomb
        of some great Lydian king,
        for being poor my gravestone is small,
        yet still too much for me.

380   ON THE GIRL GORGO
        As she lay dying in her dear mother's arms,
        Gorgo wept and whispered her last words:

        "Stay with my father,
        and on a better day bear a second daughter
        who will care for you when you are old."

381   ENCIRCLED WOMAN
        I am possessed by the fierce noise
        all around me
        of the purple, tormented sea.

382   HUMAN BANKRUPTCY
        I who lie here, Brotachos of Gortyn, was born in
            Krete,
        and I did not come here for death but weighty
            business.

383   SACRED HEALTH
        Not even lucid wisdom
        will give you joy
        when sacred health is gone.

384   FLUX
        If you are a simple mortal, do not speak
        of tomorrow or how long this man may be
        among the happy, for change comes suddenly
        like the shifting flight of a dragonfly.

385   GREEN
The birds of spring
are the green-necked
singing nightingales.

386   ON DEMIGODS
Born half-divine and sons of mighty gods,
not even these, living in ancient times,
came to old age unscorned and without painful
hardships—nor did they escape from doom.

387   ON AN ATHENIAN DAUGHTER GIVEN
TO A FOREIGN PRINCE IN LAMPSAKOS
This dust lies on Archedike, daughter of Hippias,
despot of Athens and most princely Greek of his
    day.
Although a daughter, wife, sister and mother of
    tyrants,
she never yielded to snobbery; her heart was
    humble.

388   PASSAGE OF TIME
One thousand years, ten thousand years
are but a tiny dot,
the smallest segment of a point,
an invisible hair.

389   ACCOMPLISHMENTS
Without the gods
a man or city can do nothing.
Only God knows everything, and man
suffers for what he does.

There is no evil
man may not expect, and soon
God wipes away the few things
he may have done.

Lasos

Born about 545 B.C. at Hermione in the Argolid
of the Peloponnesos, Lasos lived at Athens under
the patronage of Hipparchos, where he introduced
competitions in dithyrambic composition and was
rivaled by Simonides in this genre.

The flute player Skopelinos taught
Pindar the flute, and finding his
pupil of exceptional ability, passed
him on to Lasos of Hermione to
learn the lyre.

THOMAS MAGISTER, *Life of Pindar*

Lasisms: sophistries as the sophistries
or entangled arguments of Lasos.

HESYCHIOS, *Glossary*

◇◆◇◆◇◆◇◆◇◆◇◆◇◆◇◆◇◆◇◆◇◆◇◆◇◆◇◆◇

390   TO THE HERMIONIAN DEMETER
I sing of Demeter and the kore Persephone,
    wife of Klymenos,
and I lead
a choral hymn of honey voices
with all the low notes in the Aiolian harmony.

Theognis

*Born in Megara in 544 B.C., Theognis was a
member of the embattled aristocracy. He was in
exile for part of his life, but returned home at some
time. He lived until at least 480 B.C. The subjects
of his poetry seem to have been chiefly two: the
vicissitudes of an aristocrat fallen on evil populist
times and the moral reflections appropriate to such
experience, and the vicissitudes of the poet's
affections—chiefly directed toward one Kyrnos.
However much out-of-balance one may find
Theognis' antediluvian social and moral views, his
vivid expression of keen experience ranks him
among the supreme elegists surviving from the
Lyric Age.*

*The corpus of poems traditionally assigned to
Theognis (about 1,400 lines) by no means wholly
belongs to him. Much of it consists of imitations and
copies of earlier poets (some of this may be by
Theognis) and of Theognis himself. The collection
may have arisen as a useful handbook of after-
dinner poetry for the man who did not care to produce
his own. The poems addressed to Kyrnos have the
greatest likelihood of Theognidean authorship. The
contents of the collection may be classified as
follows: 1) autobiography; 2) preludes, hymns,
epitaphs, etc.; 3) erotic and convivial verse; 4)
gnomic or "wisdom" poetry: gather-ye-rosebud
sermons, class propaganda, praise of wealth and
dispraise of poverty, expression of aristocratic moral
code—especially the virtues of courage, resignation
and fidelity.*

We also have a witness in the poet
Theognis, a citizen of Megara, Sicily,
who said: "In a difficult dispute, a
trustworthy man is equal to gold
and silver."

PLATO, *Laws*

[142]

Theognis wrote exhortations; but
scattered among them were dis-
gusting, pederastic love poems and
pieces repugnant to a virtuous life.

The Suda Lexicon

This poet is concerned with no
other matter than the virtues and
vices of man, and his poetry is a
study of man just as a treatise on
horsemanship written by an expert
horseman studies horses.

STOBAIOS, Anthology

The epic verse of Empedokles and
Parmenides, the *Theriaka (Venom-
ous Bites)* and the *Gnomologies* of
Theognis are prose works which
borrow from poetry the use of its
meter and high tone, as if it were
a carriage, to avoid going prosai-
cally on foot.

PLUTARCH, How the Young Should
Listen to Poetry

391   SHADOWS

Fools and children you are, mankind! You mourn
the dead and not the dying flower of youth.

392   EUGENICS

In breeding donkeys, rams or horses, we seek out
the thoroughbred to get a good strain,
my Kyrnos. Yet now the noblest man will marry
the lowest daughter of a base family,
if only she brings in money. And a lady
will share her bed with a foul rich man,
preferring gold to pedigree. Money is all.
Good breed with bad and race is lost
to riches. Don't wonder our city's blood is polluted
when noble men will couple with upstarts.

393   LIBERATION

Death, friend Kyrnos, is better to the poor
    than a life cursed with painful poverty.

394   POVERTY

Nothing destroys a good man quicker than
        poverty:
    not malarial fever, Kyrnos, nor old age.
Better to hurl oneself into the abysmal sea
    or over a blunt cliff—than be a victim
of poverty. The poor man can do or say nothing
    worthwhile. Even his mouth is gagged.

395   A LOOSE VESSEL

A ripe young wife and an old husband
make a very sad conjunction.
She is like a ship. Her wild rudder
doesn't respond to him.
Her anchors don't hold.
Often she slips her moorings altogether
to enter at night in another port.

396   TO KYRNOS, A REPROACH

I gave you wings to fly looming high and easy
    over unboarded sea and the entire earth.
At every meal and banquet you will be present
    on the lips of guests. Graceful young men
will sing of you in limpid lovely notes
    to the clean piping of the flutes.
When you go under the dark vaults of earth
    to the mournful chambers of sad Hell,
even when you lie dead you will not lose
    your glory. Your name will be recalled
among men always, Kyrnos. You will wheel high
    over the mainland and Greek islands
and cross the unharvested sea pulsing with fish,
    not by horse but carried to those who love you

in the gifts of Muses capped in violet flowers.
    You will be like a song to the living
as long as there is sun, earth. Yet you ignore me
    and trick me as if I were a child.

397   A SEAMAN'S SORROW
    I heard the sharp cry of the bird, O son of
        Polypas,
      who came to men with the message to plow
    in good season; and it wounded my heart black
      that others own my flowering lands,
    and not for me are mules dragging the curved
        plow,
      now, in my exile, on the wretched sea.

398   WORDS OF A BEARDED MAN
    RECLINING ON A COUCH
    O beautiful boy, I crave you more than any man.
      Stand where you are and hear my few words.

399   GOOD WILL WASTED
    I knew it before and know it better now:
      don't wait for thanks from the lower classes.

400   HIS FAIRNESS
    I will blame no enemy who is a good man
      nor praise a friend who may be vile.

401   OUR COURSE
    Best of all things—is never to be born,
    never to know the light of sharp sun.
    But being born, then best
    to pass quickly as one can through the gates of
      Hell,
    and there lie under the massive shield of earth.

402   THE WANDERER

I have spent long days in the land of Sicily, and
    walked
    through the vineyards of the Euboian plain;
saw the city of Sparta shining by the reedy
    Eurotas.
Everywhere people took me into their homes
yet my heart found no pleasure in foreign kindness.
No place is as precious as one's homeland.

403   THE ATHLETE

Blessed is the man who knows how to make love
    as one wrestles in a gym,
and then goes home happy to sleep the day
    with a delicious young boy.

404   GOOD AND EVIL

Easier to make bad out of good than good out of
    bad.
    Don't try to teach me. I am too old to learn.

405   A CITY IN TRAVAIL

Kyrnos, the city is pregnant, and I fear it will bear
    a man who will clean up our outrageous pride.
The people are still well behaved, but the leaders
    plunge along a course of vile corruption.

Apollodoros

*Active during the late sixth
century* B.C.

Under these omens Pindar turned to
the art of poetry, his teacher being
either Lasos, as said before, or the
Athenian Agathokles or Apollodoros.
We are told about Apollodoros that
when he was the leader of the cyclic
chorus, he had to leave the city and
entrusted the training of the chorus
to Pindar, still a boy, who did so well
as to become known throughout
the area.

EUSTATHIOS, Introduction to Pindar

✦✦✦✦✦✦✦✦✦✦✦✦✦✦✦✦✦✦✦✦✦✦✦✦✦

406   WHO?
Who can be coming to the edge
of my gates
at this black hour of night?

Hipparchos

Hipparchos was the younger brother of Hippias, Tyrant of Athens (who succeeded his father Peisistratos in 527 B.C.). He was as it were the commissar of culture during his brother's reign, and was responsible for much of Athens' rapid advance in the arts. The frivolous decadence of his private life ended when he was assassinated by Harmodios and Aristogeiton in 514 B.C.

Because of their esteem and age, Hippias and Hipparchos, not their half-brothers, held the reins of power, and since Hippias was the elder and by nature a clever politician, he was virtual ruler. On the other hand, Hipparchos was childlike, amorous and a friend of the arts. It was he who brought Anakreon, Simonides and other poets to Athens.

ARISTOTLE, *Constitution of Athens*

A great light was born in Athens when Hipparchos was slaughtered by Aristogeiton and Harmodios.

SIMONIDES, *Inscription for Statues of Tyrannicides*

Hipparchos set up statues of Hermes on the roads between the city and every community in Attica ... so that his citizens would not most admire the wise sayings inscribed at Delphi, such as "Know yourself" and "Nothing in excess," but rather be guided by the wisdom of himself, Hipparchos. Thus they would read them and partake of his wisdom while going back and forth to their farms and homes, and so become enlightened men.

PLATO, *Hipparchos*

❖❖❖❖❖❖❖❖❖❖❖❖❖❖❖❖❖❖❖❖❖❖❖❖❖❖❖❖

407 INSCRIPTION FROM A STATUE OF HERMES
This will recall Hipparchos:
As you walk think of the good.

408 INSCRIPTION FROM A STATUE OF HERMES
This will recall Hipparchos:
Never doublecross a friend.

Korinna

This Boiotian poet was probably a contemporary of Pindar, but it is also possible that she lived in the late third century B.C. Until the papyrus finds of this century, she was known only in the scantiest of fragments. Her works included narrative choral lyrics intended for an audience of women, on such subjects as the Seven Against Thebes. Her diction and meter are simple, her dialect chiefly Boiotian.

Daughter of Acheloodoros and Hippokrateia, of Thebes or Tanagra; a pupil of Myrtis and a lyric poet. It is reported that she gained victory five times over Pindar in poetry competitions. She wrote five books as well as Inscriptions and Lyric Nomes.

The *Suda Lexicon*

When Pindar the poet competed at Thebes he ran into ignorant judges, and was defeated five times by Korinna. To show the judges' bad taste, Pindar called Korinna a pig.

AELIANUS, *Historical Miscellanies*

When Pindar was still young and proud of his mastery of language, Korinna censured him for his poor taste.

PLUTARCH, *Glory of Athens*

◇◆◇◆◇◆◇◆◇◆◇◆◇◆◇◆◇◆◇◆◇◆◇◆◇◆◇◆◇◆◇

409   ON HERSELF

I Korinna am here to sing the courage
of heroes and heroines in old myths.

To daughters of Tanagra in white robes,
I sing. And all the city is delighted
with the clean water of my plaintive voice.

410   THE CONTEST OF HELIKON
AND KITHAIRON
Kithairon sang of cunning Kronos
and sacred Rheia who stole her son
Zeus, mighty among immortals.

Then the Muses asked the gods to put
their ballot stones in the urn of
gold. All stood up and Kithairon won

the greater part. Hermes shouted loud,
at once proclaiming sweet victory.
The gods adorned his brow with flowers,

and Kithairon rejoiced. But Helikon
was stunned with bitter rage, and tore
a massive boulder from the mountain;

insanely he shouted and lobbed the rock
down on thousands of mortals below.

411   HERMES
When he sailed into the harbor
his ship became a snorting horse.
Hermes ravished the white city
while the wind like a nightingale
sang with his whirling war-axe.

412   ROUT OF THE ERETRIAN FLEET
For you alone, Tanagra,
Hermes came to fight
with his naked fists.

413   ON MYRTIS
Although I was her pupil,

Even I reproach Myrtis
of the crystalline voice.

She was a mere woman poet,
yet she challenged Pindar.

414   ON HERSELF
Will you sleep forever? There was a time,
Korinna, when you were not a loafer.

Telesilla

Fifth-century B.C. *poet of Argos.
She wrote hymns to the gods,
mainly for women.*

No less renowned than these collective
deeds is the battle in which the
Spartan king Kleomenes was driven
from Argos (with his men) by the
poet Telesilla.

PLUTARCH, Feminine Virtue

Above the theater is a temple of
Aphrodite. And in front of the
pedestal of the goddess is a slab
engraved with a figure of Telesilla,
the writer of songs. . . . Telesilla was
famous among women for her poetry
but still more famous for the following deed: [her defeat of the Spartans].

PAUSANIAS, Description of Greece (Argos)

❖❖❖❖❖❖❖❖❖❖❖❖❖❖❖❖❖❖❖❖❖❖❖❖❖

415   REFUGE FROM RAPE
       O Artemis and your virgin girls,
       come to us. Run swiftly
       to escape the hunter Alpheus.

416   SONG TO APOLLO
       O the sun-loving Apollo!

Timokreon

Born on Rhodes, active during first half of fifth century B.C. *He sided with the Persians in the wars and visited their king. Timokreon, who crossed poetic swords with Simonides, was reputed to be a glutton. He composed lyrics and elegies.*

When Timokreon became the guest of the Persian king, he took full advantage of the food offered him. Once, when the king asked why he was stuffing himself, he answered, "So I can give a great number of Persians a sound thrashing." The next day he defeated a large number of them, one by one, and then stood beating the air. He explained to his astonished host that he had all these blows to spare if any one would come on for more.

ATHENAIOS, *Doctors at Dinner*

After drinking and eating and slandering to my heart's content, I now lie here, Timokreon of Rhodes.

SIMONIDES

◇◇◇◇◇◇◇◇◇◇◇◇◇◇◇◇◇◇◇◇◇◇◇◇◇◇◇◇◇◇◇◇

417   THE SOURCE

Blind money, I wish you were banished
from coastal plains and the sea,
from the deep continent,
and made your home on Acheron's shore
in black Tartaros.
For all the malevolence in man
is caused by you.

[154]

Lamprokles

Active at Athens in early fifth century B.C., *he composed dithyrambs and hymns, and was an influential teacher of music.*

Pythokleides was a musician of solemn music, a Pythagorian who taught Agathokles, the teacher of Lamprokles, the teacher of Damon.*

SCHOLIAST, *on Plato*

In the *History of Harmony*, Aristoxenos claims that the Mixolydian mode was invented by Pythokleides, the flute player. Lysis states that Lamprokles of Athens, understanding that this mode has a disjunction . . . arranged it to proceed from B to B.

PLUTARCH, *On Music*

418   ON ATHENA

City-destroying Pallas,
wonderful captain in battle,
constant champion of war,
virgin, child of great Zeus,
you tame unbroken stallions.

* The teacher of Perikles and Socrates.

Pindaros (Pindar)

The prince of choral poets was born in 518 B.C. at Kynoskephalai in Boiotia, of an aristocratic family. He was educated in his craft chiefly at Athens. In the course of his career he established connections with leading families in many parts of the Greek world. (The relationship between poet and patron during this period, remarks Hermann Fränkel, should be understood within the tradition of the exchange of gifts by guest-friends, rather than treated as a sheerly commercial link.) He went to Sicily in 476 B.C. and was welcomed both by Hieron of Syracuse and by Theron of Akragas. At least from this time onward Pindar found himself on occasion in competition with Simonides and Bakchylides, and was not always the winner: Bakchylides was commissioned instead of Pindar to write an epinikion for Hieron in 468. Pindar died at eighty in 438 B.C.

The works of Pindar comprised seventeen books, including nearly all choral genres. Only the four books of his epinikian odes have survived in substantial completeness, but the fragments of others fill some eighty pages in Bowra's edition.

The style of Pindar is dense and highly personal, blended from several dialects. His viewpoint is that of an aristocratic conservative, both in religion and politics. The epinikion for Pindar is above all a religious celebration of the glories of god and hero, and (as it were incidentally) their reflection in the achievements of his aristocratic contemporaries.

Pindar has had deeper influence on subsequent literature than any other Greek lyric poet. The modern ode at its greatest is chiefly the descendant of Pindar. But, as Bowra says, "He was capable . . . at times, of a sublimity to which there is no parallel."

A delight to strangers and loved by
friends, Pindar was servant of the
sweet-voiced Muses.

PLATO

[156]

In lyric poetry would you prefer to be Bakchylides
rather than Pindar? And in tragedy Ion of Chios
rather than—Sophokles? It is true that Bakchylides
and Ion are faultless and entirely elegant writers
of the polished school, while Pindar and Sophokles,
although at time they burn everything before them
as it were in their swift career, are often extinguished
unaccountably and fail most lamentably. But would
anyone in his sense regard all the compositions of
Ion put together as an equivalent for the single play
of the *Oidipous* [or all the works of Bakchylides
as equal to a single ode of Pindar's?]

"LONGINUS," *On the Sublime*

Whoever labors to be Pindar's equal,
Iulus, mounts on wings that are fastened with wax,
Daidalos-fashion, and will give his name to
        glittering water.

As a river roars down a mountain, swollen
by showers of rain, spilling over its banks,
so Pindar rages and the deep of his voice
        pours ever onward,

worthy of the laurel sacred to Apollo,
whither he is tumbling freshly minted words
through frenzied hymns, carried along on meters
        free and unruly . . .

HORACE, *Odes*

Of the nine lyric poets Pindar is by far the greatest,
in virtue of his inspired magnificence, the beauty
of his thoughts and figures, the rich exuberance
of his language and matter and his rolling flood of
eloquence, characteristics which, as Horace rightly
held, make him inimitable.

QUINTILIAN

Pindar lies in the earth, this Pierian trumpet, strong
forger of pure hymns, whose song when heard made
one think a swarm of bees had come from the
Muses to fashion it in the chamber of Kadmos'
bride, Harmony.

ANTIPATROS OF SIDON, *P.A.*

It was during the quadrennial festival
[Pythian games] with its procession of oxen that,
as a well-loved child, I was first wrapped in
swaddling clothes.

PINDAR, Fragment

A chosen herald of wise speech, I was raised by the
Muses for Hellas. I am proud that my race and
my home are in Thebes, a city of chariots.

PINDAR, Dithyramb for Thebes

419   ECLIPSE

God has in his power
to make dazzling unmixed light
spring from the somber depths
of evening. He can also
enclose the white explosion of day
under the gloom of black clouds.

420   SINGING DANCE*

Follow the curving line of melody,
and in contest
dance frenetically to imitate
the Amyklian hound or a wild unbroken horse.

And move your body
as a hound flies across the windy plain of Dotia
to kill a horned deer
who, in desperate dance,
bobs her head and neck convulsively
to either side.

* Also attributed to Simonides.

421   OLYMPIAN ODE XII

For Ergoteles of Himera, winner of
the long distance run, 472 B.C., now
exiled from Knossos.

O daughter of liberating Zeus, I beseech you,
O saviour Fortune, guard the strength of Himera.
At sea you pilot our speeding ships,
and on land the erupting wars and assemblies
depend on your will. For men's hopes splash high,
break low as they toss through an ocean of lies.

No man of the earth has ever encountered
a sure sign from God of things to come. The future
is blind to him. It teases
his judgment: as the reversal of delight;
or as after suffering a surge of pain
the sudden turning from gloom to meadows of joy.

Son of Philanor, like a cock who fights only at
     home,
even your legs' splendor might be dull
had civil strife among bitter men
not expelled you from your homeland, Knossos.
Now, Ergoteles, garlanded at Olympia
and twice festooned at Pytho and at the Isthmos,
you honor the Hot Springs of the Nymphs—here
     at your new home, Himera.

422   AFTERLIFE IN ELYSIUM

For them the sun shines at full strength—while we
     here walk in night.
The plains around their city are red with roses
and shaded by incense trees heavy with golden
     fruit.
And some enjoy horses and wrestling, or table
     games and the lyre,
and near them blossoms a flower of perfect joy.
Perfumes always hover above the land

from the frankincense strewn in deep-shining fire
of the gods' altars.

And across from them the sluggish rivers of black
night
vomit forth a boundless gloom.

423 OLYMPIAN ODE XI
To the Lokrian boy Agesidamos,
winner in the boxing, 476 B.C.

There is a time when men most need
winds; there is a time for waters from the sky,
for raindrops, daughters of the cloud.
But if by effort a man is victorious, sweet songs
foretell later fame,
and are a pledge for remembrance of great achievements.

Abundant is the praise waiting for Olympian
victory, and my lips are pleased
to shepherd these words.
Yet only through God can wisdom blossom in a
man's soul.
So know this, Agesidamos,
for you, son of Archestratos, for your boxing
triumph I will raise a sweet song to add radiance
to your olive wreath of gold,
and speak of the West Wind Lokrians, your people.
Let us acclaim him here, Muses. I warrant
you will not be received coldly like strangers,
nor find bluntness to lovely things,
but wisdom and excellent spearmen. For neither
the fiery brown fox
nor raucous lion can change his nature given from
birth.

424 LAMENT
The stars and the rivers
and waves call you back.

425   GLORIOUS ATHENS

O shining city, festooned in violets, draped in song,
you are the marble strength of all Hellas, glorious
    Athens, sacred citadel.

426   OLYMPIAN ODE III

To Theron of Akragas in Sicily,
winner in the chariot race, 466 B.C.

I shall honor glorious Akragas and please the
    Dioskouroi, kind to strangers,
and Helen of the lovely hair,
when I have raised a hymn of Olympic victory for
    Theron and his stallions
of the never-tiring hooves. The Muses were faithful
    as I found a shining virgin mode
to link Dorian rhythms with the speech

of celebration. The olive wreath on his flowing
    locks moves me
to my God-appointed duty
to blend clamoring flutes and the lyre's supple voice
    with my pattern of words,
all for Ainesidamos' son. And Pisa bids me speak
    out. From Pisa
come heavenly songs to man

and to the victor. The upright Aitolian judge of
    Greeks, obeying Herakles' ancient laws,
loops the gray glory of the olive
over the hero's brow and locks. Long ago
    Amphitryon's son carried the silver olive tree
from the shadowy springs of the Danube,
to be the handsomest symbol of the Olympian
    games.

With candid heart he persuaded the Hyperboreans,
    people of Apollo;
he begged them for a tree for Zeus' garden
to bring refreshing shade to all men, and crown
    their valor.

Already the altars were hallowed for his father;
 and the mid-month moon,
riding in her gold cart, illumined the round eye

of evening. He established the fair judging for the
 great fifth-year games
by the overhanging banks of holy Alpheus River.
But the valley of Kronian Pelops was not yet
 verdant with beauty of trees.
He thought his garden, naked of green, must suffer
 the sun's dagger rays.
So his spirit moved him to journey

to Istrian land. There, Leto's daughter, driver of
 horses,
welcomed him as he came from ridges and mazy
 gullies of Arkadia
when, at Eurysteus' command, his doomed ties with
 Zeus drove him on his mission
to bring back the gold-horned doe that Taygeta
 one day wrote down
to be sacrificed to Artemis Orthosia.

Chasing the doe, he saw the distant land behind
 the cold north wind
and stood in wonder at the trees.
A sweet desire burned in him to plant them at the
 finish-mark of the twelve-lap track
of horses. And now he comes graciously to the
 festival, with the godlike
twin sons of deep-girdled Leda.

At Olympos he had charged those future stars to
 guide the wonderful games
where men's courage and chariot-speed
are tested. My heart impels me to say that glory
 has come to Theron
and the children of Emmenos as a gift from the
 horsemen Dioskouroi. Among all mortals
they drew near the gods through lavish feasts

and true reverence for the mysteries.
If water is best of all things, and gold the dearest
    possession,
then Theron's virtues touch the uttermost realm
    of excellence,
reaching Herakles' pillars. Beyond, the world is
    untracked
by wise or foolish. There I will not venture, being
    no fool.

Bakchylides

*A contemporary, possibly younger, of Pindar,
Bakchylides was born, like his uncle Simonides, on
the island Keos in the Kyklades. He too took part
in the dithyrambic competitions at Athens and
accompanied his uncle to Sicily around 476 B.C. He
was reportedly exiled to the Peloponnesos at some
time in his life. Like Simonides and Pindar, he wrote
for numerous patrons throughout Greece. Until 1896
there survived of Bakchylides only half as many
lyric fragments as those of Simonides. But in that
year a papyrus-find of fourteen epinikia and six
dithyrambs was made in Egypt. Among lyric poets
Bakchylides is now second only to Pindar in state
of preservation. Fragments remain of other genres
of Bakchylides' choral lyrics.*

*The language of Bakchylides is chiefly a combination
of Homeric and Doric—a version of the "standard"
international choral language. His style is on the
whole much more direct and penetrable than
Pindar's, but his diction is distinguished by an
abundance of ornamental compounds, many of them
newly coined.*

Pindar had a feud with Bakchylides,
and compares himself to an eagle and
Bakchylides to a jackdaw.

SCHOLIAST, *On Pindar*

In this ode (*Pastor cum traheret*)
Horace imitates Bakchylides.

PORPHYRIO, *On an Ode of Horace*

There are nine Lyric Poets: Alkman,
Alkaios, Sappho, Stesichoros, Ibykos,
Anakreon, Simonides, Bakchylides
and Pindar.

EUSTATHIOS, *Introduction to Pindar*

[164]

It seems that the finest and most famous
works of the ancients were also induced by
exile. The Athenian Thucydides composed his
history of the war between Athens and the
Peloponnesians near Skapte Hyle in Thrace.
Xenophon wrote at Skyllos in Elis. The poet
Bakchylides (from Keos) wrote in the Peloponnesos.

PLUTARCH, *On Exile*

427   PEACE

Only great peace
brings wealth to men
and a flowering of honey-throated song,
and to the gods
ox-thighs burning and long-haired sheep
flaming yellow on the sculpted altars,
and to the young
a love of wrestling and the flute
and Bakchic dance.

In the iron-covered shield
the brown spider hangs his web.
The sharpened spear and double-edge sword
are flaked with rust.
The noise of the brass trumpet is dead,
and the honey of our dawnsleep
is not dried from our eyelids.
Streets clamor with happy outdoor banquets,
and the lovely hymns sung by children
spring like fire up into the bright air.

428   THE WEST WIND

On his farmland Eudemos built this sanctuary
    to the Zephyr,
kind breeze among the harsh gales,

for when the farmer prayed,
the wind awoke briskly
helping him winnow good wheat from the chaff.

429   HERAKLES: A DITHYRAMB
I must not sing of you now,
O Pythian Apollo (though
the lovely-throned Urania
sent me a gold ship from Pieria
cargoed with famous hymns) if you are hunting
far by the flowering bank of the Hebros
or delighting in the soft song
of the long-necked swan.
Before you come to cull
the bloom of paeans
which the Delphian dancers
chant loudly by your shining temple,

we will sing of Amphitryon's
brave son who fled the city
of Oichalia gutted by flames;
who came to that wavewashed cape
(where he was sacrificing nine deep-roaring bulls
to the Kenaian Zeus of the broad clouds,
a pair to the seagod who lifts
salt waters and punishes earth,
and a never-yoked high-horned ox
to chaste Athena of the fierce glance)
when a dread wargod wove
a terrible poisonous weapon of blood

for Deianeira: she had learned
the sorrowful news
that the fearless son of Zeus
was sending white-armed Iole
to his luminous rooms to become his bride.
O doomed insane wife! Why did she plot
disaster! Relentless envy
drove her against

the black veil of future
on that day she took
(on the flowering bank of the Evenos)
the star-cursed gift* from the centaur Nessos.

430   IDAS WINS MARPESSA

One day in spacious Sparta
goldhaired girls
danced to a song
when courageous Idas
led Marpessa of the violet braids
to his own rooms
after eluding death.
Poseidon the sealord
gave him a chariot
and horses equal to the wind,
and sent him to the handsome city of Pleuron
and to the son of Ares of the gold shield.†

431   THESEUS: A DITHYRAMB

A blue-prowed ship was knifing the open sea
off Krete, carrying battle-fierce Theseus
and fourteen glorious
young Ionian men and girls.
The northerly winds slammed into
her white sails glittering far,
by grace of famous Athene of the war-aegis.
But the alarming gifts of Aphrodite,
who wears the headband of desire,
clawed at the heart of Minos,
and he could not keep his hand from a girl
and caressed her white cheek.
But Eriboia screamed
for Theseus the bronze-armored
offspring of Pandion; he looked

* The centaur's blood poisoned by Herakles' arrow in which jealous
Deianeira dipped the shirt of her husband, Herakles, thinking it a love
potion; the garment caused Herakles' death and her suicide.
  † Evenos, father of Marpessa.

and his eye rolled black
under his brows, and angry pain
pierced his heart, as he spoke:
"O son of peerless Zeus,
here you are steering
a course of shameful behavior
within your heart.
Hero, control that wanton violence.

Our powerful destiny comes from the gods,
and whichever way the scale of Justice
dips, we shall fulfill
our determined fate—whenever
it comes. So restrain
your heavy hand. Even if true
that you were conceived in the bed of Zeus
under the brow of Mount Ida
from the celebrated daughter
of Phoinix, yet I also came
into being when the daughter
of rich Pittheus lay with the sealord
Poseidon; and the violet-wreathed
daughters of Nereus gave her
a veil of gold. Therefore,
O war-king of the Knossians,
I ask you to hold back insolence
that will bring many tears.
I would never look on sweet light
of ambrosial dawn, were you to force
any of these youths or virgin
girls. Rather, we shall match
the strength of our hands, and the gods will judge."

So spoke the spear-brave hero,
and sailors stood spellbound
before his defiant courage,
but Helios' son-in-law raged in his soul
and concocted new tricks,
and spoke: "Omnipotent Zeus, Father,
hear me. If I am your son by Phoinix' daughter,
your white-armed bride,

now break swiftly from the sky
a fire-haired flash of thunder,
a sign all will know. Theseus, if Aithra
from Troizen really bore you
as son to Poseidon the earth-shaker,
go leap into the deep pelagos,
your father's chambers,
and bring back this shining
gold ornament of my hand,
my ring. Now you will know
if Kronos' son, lord of thunder
and master of all, will hear my prayers."

Zeus, mountain of strength, listened to his pure
prayer and approved; and wishing to honor
his son in great public
display, spilled down
a flash of lightning. Minos, seeing
the welcome portent, raised his arms
to the echoing sky; the battle-fierce
hero spoke: "Theseus, now you see
how shining clear are my gifts
from Zeus. Come, dive into the roar
of the open sea, and your father,
the lord Poseidon, son of Kronos,
will lift you in transcendent glory
over the land of handsome trees."
He spoke, and Theseus did not flinch.
A heart of iron, standing tall
on the solid deck he sprang,
and the deep forest of the sea
took him down kindly. Zeus' son
was inwardly amazed,
and ordered the well-made ship
to sail before the wind.
But Destiny swept them on another course.

Pummeled astern by a northern blast
the rapid vessel shot ahead
and the group of Athenian
youths trembled in fear

as their hero plunged to the water.
Tears formed in their flower-bright
eyes, as they thought of the grave danger.
But dolphins, roamers in the sea,
easily bore great Theseus
to the palace of his horseman father.
He entered the regal hall of gods.
There he looked with fearful wonder
at the beautiful daughters
of rich Nereus. From their
fabled bodies shone a glory
of fire, and ribbons of gold
were twined among their braids
as their nimble feet floated
in happy dance. He saw
in the pleasant palace
the ox-eyed Amphitrite,
his father's true majestic wife,
who wrapped round him a robe of purple linen,

and laid on his heavy mat of hair
an immaculate wreath
that one day at her marriage
cunning Aphrodite in rose garland gave her.
For men of sound mind
no labor by the gods is past belief.
Beside the ship's narrow stern Theseus came up
and how he amazed
the Knossian warlord
when he rose unwet from the sea,
a miracle to all, and on
his limbs gleamed the gift of the gods.
The bright-throned nymphs
shrieked in pristine triumph,
the sea clamored,
and those youths about him
sang a loud perfect paean!
O Lord of Delos, your heart
warmed with Kean chorales,
grant us godly blessings in all we do.

Praxilla

*Poet active about 450 B.C. at
Sikyon in the Argolid. She wrote
dithyrambs, drinking songs and
hymns.*

Praxilla was portrayed in bronze by
Lysippos, although she spoke nonsense
in her poetry.

TATIAN, *Against the Greeks*

Only a simpleton would put
cucumbers and the like on a par
with the sun and the moon.

ZENOBIOS

✧✦✧✦✧✦✧✦✧✦✧✦✧✦✧✦✧✦✧✦✧✦✧✦✧✦✧

432   OF THE SENSUAL WORLD

Most beautiful of things I leave is sunlight;
then come glazing stars and the moon's face;
then ripe cucumbers and apples and pears.

433   APPEARANCE

You gaze at me teasingly through the window:
a virgin face—and below—a woman's thighs.

434   ACHILLES

(You understood their words)

but they never reached the heart
buried in your chest.

[171]

435   THE COWARD

Under cover
a coward will strike from any side.
I warn you, friend:
watch out for his sting.
Under every rock is a lurking scorpion.

Parrhasios

*A noted painter active at Athens probably in the
second half of the fifth century* B.C. *His reported
skill in details of facial expression and in outline
drawing perhaps justified in part the* hybris *of the
epigram given below. Parrhasios was represented
as discussing painting with Sokrates in Xenophon's*
Memorabilia, *and himself wrote on the art.*

Parrhasios so systematized all art that he is known
as the lawgiver; the depiction of gods and heroes
according to his manner is followed by other
painters, as though by necessity.

QUINTILIAN, *Elements of Oratory*

Euenor was the father and teacher of the great
painter Parrhasios.

PLINY, *Natural History*

436   PERFECTION IN ART

I say, even if those who hear are unbelieving,
I affirm that my hand has discovered the limits
   of art.
Though nothing is flawless in the world of men,
now the mark is fixed and cannot be surpassed.

437   ON A PAINTING OF HERAKLES
FOR WHICH THE GOD POSED

Now you may see the god—exactly as he was,
   coming to me Parrhasios in my dream.

Hippon

Natural philosopher, probably from Samos, was active in the latter half of the fifth century B.C. He revived and modified the view that water was the source of all things.

Kratinos also accuses Hippon of impiety.
SCHOLIAST, *On Clement of Alexandria*

Hippon of Rhegium declared that the elements were cold (water) and heat (fire), and that fire, when made from water, overcame the power of its author and formed the world.
HIPPOLYTOS, *Against Heresies*

Because of the impoverished nature of his thinking, Hippon is not worthy of being included with those philosophers who hold water to be an element or first principle.
ARISTOTLE, *Metaphysics*

438   ON THE ATHEIST PHILOSOPHER
FROM RHEGIUM, CALABRIA

Here is the grave of Hippon. When he died
fate made him equal to the eternal gods.

Melanippides

A famous dithyrambic poet of his time. Born on Melos (and hence a Dorian) he was active during the middle of the fifth century B.C. and died at the court of Perdikkas in Macedonia. A comic poet attributed to Melanippides the first innovations which led to the decadence of choral lyric. One innovation was the introduction of lyric solos into the dithyramb. In addition to dithyrambs, Melanippides wrote epics, elegies and epigrams.

Like his grandafther he was a lyric poet. He made
great innovations in the dithyramb and spent
part of his life at the court of the Macedonian king
Perdikkas, where he died. He wrote lyric poems
and dithyrambs.

The *Suda Lexicon*

"Tell me, Aristodemos," he asked, "are there any
men whose art you esteem?" "Yes," he said. "Tell
us their names," Sokrates asked. "For the epic
I especially admire Homer, for the dithyramb
Melanippides. . . ."

XENOPHON, *Recollections of Sokrates*

439   THE DANAÏDS
They were not shaped like handsome men
nor was their voice womanly,
but they trained naked
driving in chariots about the sunny
treelands. Often
they were happy in hunting;
often they sought the holy tear
of the dripping frankincese,
the good smell of dates
or smooth seeds of Syrian cassia.

Timotheos

*Timotheos was born at Miletos around 450 B.C.
and died around 360 B.C., possibly in Macedon,
whither he (like his friend Euripides) had been
invited by King Archelaos. The most famous lyric
poet of his time, Timotheos was also (according to
some tastes ancient and modern) one of the most
pernicious. His musical innovations were striking,
and carried such weight (with Euripides, for
example) that they contributed mightily to the
decay of the verbal side of the ode. The language
in his surviving fragments is often preposterously
artificial and periphrastic. Yet the long papyrus
fragment on the defeat of the Persians (published
in 1903) includes a jarringly "realistic" imitation
of a Persian speaking in broken Greek. His works
included nomes, dithyrambs, hymns, encomia, etc.*

When Timotheos was hissed because he seemed to
be an innovator and rebel against the laws of
music, Euripides asked him to take heart, for soon
the theater audience would acclaim him.

PLUTARCH, *Should Old Men Govern?*

Here the Spartans hung the lyre of Timotheos of
Miletos, after censuring him for having added four
new strings to the traditional seven in the art
of singing to the lyre.

PAUSANIAS, *On Sparta*

If there had been no Timotheos, we would not
have much of our lyric poetry, and if there had
been no Phrynis there would have been no
Timotheos.

ARISTOTLE, *Metaphysics*

440   TO APOLLO

Sun, your phosphorescent rays pin fire
across the eternal firmament.
Snap a far-hunting arrow against our enemies,
O careering Healer to whom we cry!

Platon (Plato)

Born about 429 B.C. *in Athens and died in 347. He was a disciple of Sokrates, later the founder of the Academy, and in effect the father of Western philosophy. If he was in fact the author of the epigrams attributed to him, his* Phaidros *and* Symposion *may provide the spiritual link between his amatory epigrams and his philosophical works. "Hesperos" has been called the most perfect of all epigrams. Shelley prefixed it to his "Adonais."*

You were the most accomplished
stylist of the fine Attic tongue, and
all Greek literature has no greater
voice than yours. Inspired Plato, you
were the first to contemplate ethics
and life, looking to God and heaven.
You combined the high thinking of
Pythagoras with the cutting spirit of
Sokrates, and were a beautiful
monument of their solemn dissension.

ANONYMOUS, *Palatine Anthology*

If Apollo had not given Plato to
Greece, how could he cure men's
souls by writings? While Apollo's
son Asklepios heals the human body,
Plato heals the immortal soul.

DIOGENES LAERTIOS, *Palatine Anthology*

The golden bough of Plato's poems,
forever divine, and shining with
virtue.

from the *Stephanos of Meleagros, 1st proem*

441   HESPEROS
       You were the Morning Star among the living.
       In death, O Evening Star, you light the dead.

442   LOVE POEM
       My child—Star—you gaze at the stars,
       and I wish I were the firmament
       that I might watch you with many eyes.

443   THE APPLE
       I am an apple, and one who loves you
       tossed me before you. O yield to him,
       dear Xanthippe! Both you and I decay.

444   LESSON FROM THE ACADEMY
       I throw this apple before you.
       Take it—if you love me purely,
       and give up your virginity.

       Yet if you will not love me
       keep the apple—and think
       how long the beauty lasts.

445   SOKRATES TO HIS LOVER
       As I kissed Agathon my soul swelled to my lips,
       where it hangs, pitiful, hoping to leap across.

446   THE FAMOUS COURTESAN LAÏS
       DEDICATES A MIRROR TO APHRODITE
       I Laïs who laughed scornfully at Hellas,
       who kept a swarm of young lovers at my door,
       I lay my mirror before the Paphian,
       for I will not see myself as I am now,
       and cannot see myself as once I was.

       [179]

447   ON LOVING ALEXIS

I barely whispered that Alexis was handsome
and now all the loose hounds goggle at him.
My heart, why do you show the dogs a bone?
Soon you'll suffer, as when you lost Phaidros.

448   SOKRATES TO ARCHEANASSA

My girlfriend was Archeanassa from Kolophon
and her wrinkles are scars of a sour love.
Pain, horror. On her first voyage she loved
a graceful young man, and passed through fire.

449   MODESTY

Aphrodite cried at Knidos when she saw Aphrodite:
    O Zeus! Where did Praxiteles see me naked?

450   ON TIME

Time brings everything; and dragging years alter
    names and forms, nature and even destiny.

451   DEATH AT SEA

Sailors be free of disaster on land and sea,
for you are passing by a sailor in his grave.

452   PINDAR

A delight to strangers and loved by friends,
Pindar labored for the sweet-voiced Muses.

453   SAPPHO

Some say nine Muses—but count again.
Behold the tenth: Sappho of Lesbos.

454   IN THE PINE GROVE
Sit below the long needles of the resonant pine
as its branches shudder in the western winds.
A shepherd's piping by the loquacious river
will lay heavy sleep on your spellbound eyelids.

455   PAN
Be still, green cliff of the Dryads. Be still,
springs bubbling among rocks, and confused noisy
bleating of the ewes.
For it is Pan playing on his honey-voiced pipe.
His supple lips race over the clustered reeds,
while all round him
a ring of dancers spring up on joyful feet:
Nymphs of the Water and Nymphs of the Oak
    Forest.

456   ARISTOPHANES
When looking for an inviolable sanctuary,
the Graces found the soul of Aristophanes.

457   ON A DOOMED SETTLEMENT IN MEDIA
We lying here in the open plains of Ekbatana
once heard the throbbing waves of the Aigaian.
Farewell famous Eretria,
                        once our country.
Farewell Athens,
                    our neighbor by Euboia.
Farewell beloved sea!

458   CAPTIVITY IN PERSIA
We are Eretrians of Euboia, but we lie in Susa,
    and how remote, now, is our motherland!

459　ON A THIEF

You look upon a shipwrecked man. The sea killed
　me but was ashamed to strip me of my last
　garment.
It took a man's inglorious hands to rob me naked,
　a grave sacrilege for such a shabby
gown. Let the poor wretch wear it down in Hell
　where King Minos may see him in my rags.

460　EQUALITY OF DEATH

I am a sailor's tomb. Beside me lies a farmer.
　Hell is the same, under the land and sea.

461　INSCRIPTION FOR THE TOMB OF DION,
　TYRANT OF SYRACUSE

Tears were fated for Hekabe and Ilium's women
　from the day of their birth,
but Dion, just when you triumphed with famous
　works,
all your wandering hopes were cast down by the
　gods.
Now dead in your spacious city, you are honored
　by patriots—
But I was one who loved you, O Dion!

The
Hellenistic Period

EARL THOLLANDER BONNIEUX '65

Diphilos

A comic poet of Athens, born before 340 B.C., died after 289 B.C. He wrote some one hundred plays. The passage below is in iambics, and was probably taken from one of his plays for inclusion in the Greek Anthology.

462 ON THE ARGIVES

Argos may be a land of horses
but the inhabitants are wolves.

Anyte

Active about 290 B.C. Poet of Arkadia in the Peloponnesos, she wrote epigrams, mock-epitaphs and nature poems in the Doric dialect.

The many lilies of Anyte.
from the *Stephanos of Meleagros, 1st proem*

❖❖❖❖❖❖❖❖❖❖❖❖❖❖❖❖❖❖❖❖❖❖❖❖❖

463　REPOSE
Lounge in the shade of the luxuriant laurel's
beautiful foliage. And now drink sweet water
from the cold spring so that your limbs weary
with summer toil will find rest in the west wind.

464　EPITAPH OF A SLAVE
Alive, this man was Manes, a common slave.
Dead, even great Darius is not his peer.

465　ON A STATUE IN AN ORCHARD
I am Hermes. I stand in the crossroads by a windy
　belt of trees near the gray shore of the sea
where the weary traveler may rest: here a fountain
　bubbles forth a cold and stainless water.

Kallimachos

*Born about 305 B.C. in Kyrene in
North Africa. He became a schoolmaster in Alexandria, and then
cataloguer of the royal library (the
most famous library of ancient times).
He produced a systematic catalog
of the library which has been called
"the first scientific literary history."
Kallimachos was the center of a con-
troversy over the proper length of
a poem; he claimed that the long
poem was an anachronism. The
typical "learned" poet composing
for a narrow, sophisticated audience,
he was versatile, experimental and
prolific.*

*His known works include a long
but episodic narrative-didactic
poem in elegiacs, narrative hymns,
iambics, miniature epics (epyllia),
lyrics (of which little survives),
elegies, dramas (lost) and—most
important for lyric in the modern
sense—epigrams.*

The sweet myrtle of Kallimachos
is always full of harsh honey.
              from the *Stephanos of Meleagros, 1st proem*

Epitaph on Himself

You are walking by the tomb of
    Kallimachos,
who was accomplished in singing
    poems
and knew when to laugh over his wine.
                    KALLIMACHOS, *Palatine Anthology*

✧✧✧✧✧✧✧✧✧✧✧✧✧✧✧✧✧✧✧✧✧✧✧✧✧✧✧

466   EPITAPH OF A YOUNG BOY
        Here Philippos the father buried his son
        Nikoteles,
        a child of twelve and his dearest hope.

467   TWOFOLD GRIEF
        It was morning when we buried Melanippos
        and by sundown Basilo his virgin sister
        was dead by her own hand.
        She could not bear to live
        after she had placed him on the funeral pyre.
        Their father's home displayed a double sorrow,
        its lovely children gone,
        and all Kyrene watched with downcast eyes.

468   ON THE DEATH OF A POET
        They brought me word of your death,
        Herakleitos,
        and I wept for you
        remembering how often we watched the sun
        setting as we talked.

        Dear Halikarnassian friend,
        you lie elsewhere now
        and are mere ashes;
        yet your songs—your nightingales—will live,
        and never will the underworld,
        destroying everything,
        touch them with its deadly hand.

469   EPITAPH OF AN ENEMY
        Passerby, do not wish me well with your sour
            heart.
        Go away. And I shall be well by your being gone.

470   A SAILOR ON THE BEACH

Who are you, O shipwrecked stranger?
Leontichos found your corpse on the beach,
buried you in this grave
and cried thinking of his own hazardous life.
For he knows no rest:
he too roams over the sea like a gull.

Theokritos

The latest of the major Greek poets. An approximate contemporary of Kallimachos, he was born at Syracuse perhaps ca. 310 B.C. Active there, at Kos (an island in the Dodekanese), and at the court of Ptolemy II in Alexandria. He died perhaps ca. 250 B.C. As his best-known genre, the pastoral mime, suggests, he wrote for an audience of high sophistication. His Idylls (or "Little Forms") are for the most part on the borderline or outside the range of "lyric" poetry. They include works of the most diverse sort: pastoral and urban mimes (short quasi-realistic dramatic episodes), epyllia (short epic narratives), hymns, and love poetry after the manner of Sappho and Alkaios. Although "literary" Doric is his predominant dialect, Theokritos also used the Epic, Ionic and Aiolic dialects with skill. Some twenty epigrams are included in his surviving corpus. Pastoral art from Vergil to Picasso and Ravel is in his debt.

I am not the other Theokritos from
    Chios.* I am
Theokritos who wrote these poems
    and one of many
Syracusans. Son of Praxagoras and
    noble Philinna,
my muse is from my own native land.
                    THEOKRITOS, *Introductory Poem to Idylls*

✧✧✧✧✧✧✧✧✧✧✧✧✧✧✧✧✧✧✧✧✧✧✧✧✧✧✧✧✧

471   TO THE GOATHERD

Goatherd, when you turn the corner by the oaks
you'll see a freshly carved statue in fig wood.
The bark is not peeled off. It is legless, earless,

---

* A fourth-century B.C. orator and sophist.

but strongly equipped with a dynamic phallus
to perform the labor of Aphrodite.
                                    A holy hedge
runs around the precinct where a perennnial brook
spills down from upper rocks and feeds a
    luxuriance
of bay, myrtle and fragrant cypress trees.

A grape vine pours its tendrils along a branch,
and spring blackbirds echo in pure transparency
of sound to high nightingales who echo back
with pungent honey.
                            Come, sit down, and beg Priapos
to end my love for Daphnis. Butcher a young goat
in sacrifice. If he will not, I make three vows:
I will slay a young cow, a shaggy goat and a darling
lamb I am raising. May God hear you and assent.

472   DAPHNIS
        Daphnis, you lie on the earth on some leaves
        resting your tired body.
                                    The hunting stakes
        are newly set in the hills. Pan
        is on your track, and Priapos comes with saffron
            ivy
        tied about his forehead. They are heading
        for your cave. Hurry!
                            Shake off your lethargy and run!

473   OFFERINGS
        These are gifts for Pan. And Daphnis
        who pays country tunes on a warbling pipe—
        he of the milk-white skin—gave them:

        his double reed, a staff for hunting hare,
        a fawn hide and keen javelin. And a pouch
        of leather in which he once carried apples.

[191]

474   SACRIFICIAL GOAT

Morning-wet roses and the redolent thyme
are for ladies of Helikon.
                        But laurel trees
                        with black leaves
that grace the precipice at Delphi
are for you, Apollo: Pythian Healer.

The horned he-goat lowers his white body
as he grazes on the tips of sagging terebinth.
His blood will
soon spill across the altar.

475   LATE SUMMER

Many poplars and many elms shook overhead,
and close by, holy water swashed down noisily
from a cave of the nymphs. Brown grasshoppers
whistled busily through the dark foliage. Far
treetoads gobbled in the heavy thornbrake.

Larks and goldfinch sang, turtledoves were
        moaning,
and bumblebees whizzed over the plashing brook.

The earth smelled of rich summer and autumn
        fruit:
we were ankle-deep in pears, and apples rolled
all about our toes. With dark damson plums
the young sapling branches trailed on the ground.

Leonidas of Tarentum

Early third century B.C. *"One of the greatest Greek epigrammatists," says Gilbert Highet of him. Author of about one hundred epigrams in an elaborate and artificial style, mostly about the life of the poor, to which class he belonged. Much admired by the Romans, and imitated by Vergil and Propertius.*

Far from my Italian soil I lie, far
from my land of Tarentum; and
this is more bitter to me than death.
Such is the intolerable life of a
wanderer. But the Muses loved me,
and I have more honey than bitter
fruits. The name of Leonidas goes
unforgotten. His gifts from the
Muses proclaim it as long as there
is sun.

LEONIDAS OF TARENTUM,
Epitaph on Himself

476 FAIR WARNING FROM PRIAPOS

The season for sailing. Already the chattering
 swallow
returns with the slender west wind.
Meadows bloom, and the boiling waves of the
 sea,
whipped by gales, are smooth and silent.
Come then, sailor, haul in the anchors and loosen
 the hawsers
and sail with all the canvas flying.
It is Priapos, god of the harbor, who warns you
 now:
set out from this port for foreign cargoes.

477   SUMMER THIRST

Traveler, do not drink the warm water
from this pool,
all muddy from the quick mountain brook
and the intruding sheep.
Go a little further up the hill
where the heifers are grazing,
and there by a shepherd's pine
                                    you will find
bubbling up through the porous rock
a spring colder than northern snow.

Asklepiades

*Active about 270 B.C. in Alexandria.
Asklepiades was the
originator of much of the traditional imagery of love poetry, including Cupid's arrows.*

◇◇◇◇◇◇◇◇◇◇◇◇◇◇◇◇◇◇◇◇◇◇◇◇◇◇◇◇◇

478 SNOW IN SUMMER
Snow in summer on a dry tongue
   is sweet,
and after winter sweet for the sailor
   to see the spring stars,
but sweetest when one cloak shelters
   two lovers,
and the Kyprian is praised.

479 PRUDENCE
Save your maidenhead? What's the good?
My girl, down in Hades there are no lovers.
The pleasures of Kypris are for the living.
Once past Acheron, river of death,
we shall lie as bones and dust.

480 NEGRESS
Didyme plunders me with her beauty.
When I look at her I am wax over fire.
If she's black, what of it? So are coals.
When kindled, they glow like blooming roses.

481 ON A MAN-DEVOURING WHORE
Voracious Philainion bit me. The bite doesn't show
yet pain crawls in me, creeps to my very fingertips.
Love, I am drained, done in, dead! I fell half-dazed
on a viperous whore, and her embrace was death.

482   TO ZEUS

Snow, thunder, hail, blaze and blacken the earth,
shake the clouds,
kill me and I will stop,
but let me live
and I shall go on, a slave of love.
And Zeus,
Aphrodite was also your master
when you stormed as gold rain through a bridal
     window
to shower down on lovely Danaë.

Mnasalkas

Of Sikyon, flourished about 250 B.C.

The sharp needles of Mnasalkas' pines.
　　　from the *Stephanos of Meleagros, 1st proem*

✧✧✧✧✧✧✧✧✧✧✧✧✧✧✧✧✧✧✧✧✧✧✧✧✧✧✧✧✧

483　AT THE TEMPLE OF APHRODITE
Let us stand on this low beach by the crashing
　　surge
and gaze at the holy groves of the seaborn
Kyprian; at the bubbling spring under shadowy
　　poplars
where a shrilling kingfisher dips its bill.

Theodoridas

Syracusan epigrammatist of the second half of the third century B.C.

◇◆◇◆◇◆◇◆◇◆◇◆◇◆◇◆◇◆◇◆◇◆◇◆◇◆◇◆◇

484   EPITAPH OF A SAILOR
I am the tomb of a drowned sailor. Sail on.
Even while we sank, the others sped away.

Moschos

*Of Syracuse, active around 150 B.C. Pastoral poet,
to whom some half-dozen short pieces may be
assigned. The* Rape of Europa (*a short narrative*)
and the Lament for Bion *have also been attributed
to Moschos, but chronology definitely excludes the
latter.*

✧✦✦✦✦✦✦✦✦✦✦✦✦✦✦✦✦✦✦✦✦✦✦✦✦✧

485   LANDLOVER
When wind dips calmly over the blue sea
my cowardly soul stirs. My love for land
becomes a craving for the vast salt waters.
But when the ocean bottom roars, and foam boils
spitting skyward on the wild crashing waves,
I gaze at the shore and its forests, and shun
the sea. Then I love black earth and shadowy
woods where even during a blasting gale
a pine tree sings. What a wretched life
the fisherman has—with his berth a home,
the sea his labor and fish his wandering prey!
I prefer to sleep under a leafy plane
and hear the plashing of a bubbling spring
which soothes the soul and never
brings me pain.

Ariston

Lived in time to be included in Meleagros' anthology.

✧✦✧✦✧✦✧✦✧✦✧✦✧✦✧✦✧✦✧✦✧✦✧✦✧✦✧

486   A POOR SCHOLAR'S WARNING

Mice, if you come for bread, go find another hole;
I live in a humble hut.
Go to some rich man's villa
where you can nibble on fat cheese and dried
    raisins
and make a feast out of scraps.

But if you come to sharpen your teeth on my
    books
your supper will be a dull poison.

Meleagros

Lived about 140-70 B.C., at Tyros and on Kos.
As a philosopher, he wrote Cynic satirical sermons,
now lost. He collected the first serious anthology
of epigrams, and more than 130 of his own epigrams
survive; these are mainly erotic, and written in the
florid and complex "Asian" style.

◇◇◇◇◇◇◇◇◇◇◇◇◇◇◇◇◇◇◇◇◇◇◇◇◇◇◇◇◇

487   SHINING FOE

O morning star, bright enemy of love,
how slowly you turn around the world
while Demos lies warm with another
                    under her cloak.
But when my slender love lay on my chest,
how swiftly you came to stand above us,
drenching us with light that seemed to laugh
                    at our loss.

488   LOVE'S WAGES

Heavy soul, now you bellow fire,
now recover your cool breathing.
But why cry? When you harbored Eros,
you knew he would rise against you.

So be resigned to fire and snow;
you sheltered him, and this is your pay.
You must suffer now for being a fool,
as you sizzle in boiling honey.

489   MYISKOS

By Love, I swear it!
Tender are the boys whom Tyros nurtures.

[201]

Yet Myiskos is the sun,
and when he illuminates the world
bright stars fade under his light.

490   AFTER CHARYBDIS

Where are you driving me,
foul waves of love,
huge sleepless winds of jealousy,
turbulent sea of orgy?

The rudder of my heart is broken:
I drift.
Will I ever again see
the voluptuous Skylla?

491   FLOWERS FOR HELIODORA

White, white violets
with myrtle and tender narcissus;
I shall weave laughing lilies
and soft crocus and purple hyacinths
with roses, flowers of lovers.
I shall come to decorate her brow
and brighten her perfumed hair
in a fine rain of flowers.

492   LIGHT OF BEAUTY

The flowers looped in Heliodora's hair darken
but she glows brighter as the flowers fade.

493   A THIEVING SKY

Morning Star, herald of dawn: goodbye,
and come back swiftly as the Evening Star;
bring me her, clandestinely, whom you stole.

494   THE WINE CUP

The wine cup is happy. It rubbed against
warm Zenophila's erotic mouth. O bliss!
I wish she would press her lips under my lips
and in one breathless gulp drain down my soul.

495   LOVE ON THE BLUE WATER

Asklepias adores making love. She gazes at a man,
her aquamarine eyes calm like the summer seas,
and persuades him to go boating on the lake of
    love.

496   HELIODORA'S FINGERNAIL

Your fingernail, Heliodora, was grown by Eros
and sharpened by him. How else could
your mere scratching be a claw against my heart?

497   THE KISS

Your eyes are fire, Timarian, your kiss birdlime.
You look at me and I burn. You touch me and I
    stick!

498   SOLE TENURE

Zenophila, my flowering tree, you are asleep.
Though wingless, I would come like Hypnos,
and bury myself under your eyelids—
so that even sleep might not intrude,
and I alone possess you.

499   HOUR OF THE SPRING

Winter squalls are drained out of the sky,
the violet season of flowering spring smiles,
the black earth glitters under a green lawn,
swelling plants pop open with tiny petals,
meadows laugh and suck the dew of morning
while the rose unfolds.

                              The shepherd in the hills
happily blows the top notes of his pipe,
the goatherd gloats over his white kids.
Sailors race across the thrashing waves,
their canvas swollen on the harmless breeze.
Drinkers acclaim the grape-giver Dionysos,
capping their hair with flowering ivy.
Bees from the putrid carcass of a bull
work with intent care; bunched in their hive
they spill a limpid honey through the comb's
perforations.
                    All tribes of birds clamor—
kingfishers on the sea, swallows in rafters,
swans by river banks, nightingales in groves.

When saplings blossom and dry meadows revive
or shepherds pipe and shaggy flocks meander
or fleets scud on the sea and drinkers dance
or bees labor and birds dazzle the sky with song,
why can a singer not praise the lovely spring?

500   THE LAST VICTORY

I'm on the ground, cruel god, so bury your heel
        in my neck.
    I feel, God knows! your ponderous weight
and arrows of fire. Yet you can't burn me any
        more.
    Hurl your torches at my heart. All is ashes.

501   I, MELEAGROS

My nurse was the island of Tyros,
and Attic land of Syrian Gadara was
my birthplace. I was sired by Eukrates
—I, Meleagros, friend of the Muses
and first to waken to the Graces of
Menippos. A Syrian? What if I am?
Stranger, we all live in one country:
    the world.

Out of one Chaos were all men born.
In my old age I traced these letters
　　on the slab before my grave,
knowing that old men are neighbors
　　to death.
Passerby, wish me well, the talkative old man,
and you may also reach a loquacious old age.

Bion

Born in Asia Minor. Active around 100 B.C.,
mostly in Sicily, where, according to tradition,
he was poisoned by jealous rivals. Classed as a
pastoral poet, though the pastoral element is not
prominent in his surviving seventeen fragments.
The Lament for Adonis *is sometimes assigned to*
him.

Nightingales mourning in the thick
foliage, carry word to the Sicilian
springs of Arethousa that the cow-
herd Bion is dead. And with him
song and Dorian poetry have like-
wise perished.

UNKNOWN PUPIL OF BION,
from *Lament for Bion*

✧✧✧✧✧✧✧✧✧✧✧✧✧✧✧✧✧✧✧✧✧✧✧✧✧✧✧✧✧

502   HESPEROS

Evening Star, gold light of Aphrodite born in the
     foam,
Evening Star, holy diamond of the glassblue night,
you are dimmer than the moon, brighter than
     another star.
Hello, good friend!
                         I'm on my way to serenade
my shepherd love. Give me your rays in place of
     moonlight.
There was a new moon today, but quickly set.
I am no thief, no highway man to plague a
     traveler at night.
A lover I am. And those in love must be helped.

503 POLYPHEMOS

What will I do? I'll just go my way
across to that distant hill and down
again to the sandpits on the shore.
And I'll sing quietly to myself
my prayer for Galateia, who doesn't care.
Yet till the shattering end of old age
I will never once abandon sweet hope.

The
Roman Period

Philodemos the Epicurean

*Lived about 110-40/35 B.C. A
teacher and popularizer of Greek
philosophy for the Romans, he
was to influence Vergil and Horace.
Approximately twenty-five of his
epigrams survive in the Anthology.*

❖❖❖❖❖❖❖❖❖❖❖❖❖❖❖❖❖❖❖❖❖❖❖❖❖❖❖❖

504   THE PRIVATE LIFE OF PHILODEMOS
Philenis, fill our silent confidant—
the lamp—with olive dew. Then go,
and lock the stout door behind you,
for love abhors a breathing witness;
and you, sweet Xantho, let us begin . . .

Only my couch, a friend to lovers,
will know the secrets of Aphrodite.

505   AN AGELESS LOVER
Charito is more than sixty
yet her hair is still a dense forest
and no brassiere holds up the marble cones
                        of her high-pointed breasts.
Her unwrinkled flesh exhales ambrosia
                        and myriads of teasing charms.

Lovers, if you do not run from hot desire,
enjoy Charito
                and forget her many decades.

Diodoros

The poems under this name in the Anthology,
according to highest authority (Wilhelm Schmid),
can be attributed to any of three different men.
At any rate they probably belong to the period
100 B.C.-A.D. *100.*

506   THE FALL
A tiny child in the villa of Diodoros
fell headfirst from a little ladder
and broke his neck bones fatally,
but when he saw his much-loved master
running up,
he suddenly spread out his baby arms to him.

Earth, do not lie heavy on the bones
of a tiny slave child.
Be kind to Korax, who died at two.

Antipatros of Thessalonike

*Flourished at the beginning of the
Christian era. Some eighty of his
epigrams are in the* Anthology.

◇◇◇◇◇◇◇◇◇◇◇◇◇◇◇◇◇◇◇◇◇◇◇◇◇◇◇◇◇

507   MORNING GRAY

Morning gray is here, Chrysilla, and long ago
the twilight cock began to herald jealous Dawn
               and guide her by my window.
Go away, selfish bird!
You drive me out of home to the crowded chatter
   of young men.
Tithonos, you're getting old.
Why else have you chased your bedmate Dawn
so early from her couch?

508   A DOUBLE GRAVE

Neither the sea nor land may claim my body.
In this death they share me in equal parts.
The fish devoured all my flesh in the sea,
but my bones were washed up on this cold beach.

Marcus Argentarius

Lived at the beginning of the Christian era. He was probably a penniless speech teacher. "The liveliest of the Graeco-Roman epigrammatists," Gilbert Highet has said of him.

◇◇◇◇◇◇◇◇◇◇◇◇◇◇◇◇◇◇◇◇◇◇◇◇◇◇◇◇◇◇◇

509   DIALOG

"Take a hard look at scrawny Diokleia.
She's a skinny Aphrodite
                        but sweet."

"Then nothing will stand between us;
when I lie on her skinny breasts
I'll be pressing right against her heart."

510   DISCREET WITNESS

As I lay clutching Antigone's body,
my chest throbbed against her bosom,
my lips pressed into her sweet lips—

for the rest you must ask the lamp.

511   OXYMORON*

Melissa, you do everything like a bee:
when you kiss, you drip sweet honey from your
        lips;
when you ask for money,
I feel the savage wound of your sting.

* Melissa is a name and also means honeybee.

[214]

Rufinus

Lived sometime between 50 B.C. and A.D. 50.

✧✦✧✦✧✦✧✦✧✦✧✦✧✦✧✦✧✦✧✦✧✦✧✦✧✦✧

512   A LETTER FROM RUFINUS IN EPHESOS

I Rufinus wish my darling Elpis only pleasure,
    if you are happy away from me.
Yet I swear before you: I am wracked with pain
    without you in my lonely bed.
With moist eyes I go to the hill of Koressos
    or the temple of great Artemis.
Tomorrow when my city receives me, I will fly
    to greet you with a thousand blessings.

513   A NAKED BATHER

A silver-ankled girl was bathing in a brook,
    letting the water flood down
on the gold apples of her milky breasts.

When she walked, her round hips rolled and flowed
    more liquid than the water.
Her arm reached down to shield her swelling belly,
    not all—but all her hand could hide.

514   REMORSE

If women were as enticing after, as before,
no man would be bored with his wife's body.
But after love, all women are distasteful.

Apollonides

Lived sometime between 50 B.C.
and A.D. *50.*

515   THE MESSAGE

If you come to Apollo's harbor at Miletos,
bring Diogenes this desolate word:
off the island of Andros was a shipwreck,
and your son Diphilos, bloated with waves,
lies on the earth bottom of the Aigaian Sea.

Parmenion

Lived sometime between 50 B.C. and A.D. 50.

516   A DISCREET PURCHASE

Zeus bought Danaë with golden rain
and I purchase you with a gold coin.
I can't, after all, pay more than Zeus.

Nikarchos

*Alexandrian epigrammatist, prob-
ably of the first century* A.D.
*About forty of his epigrams are
in the Anthology; they are humor-
ous, and often vile.*

◇◇◇◇◇◇◇◇◇◇◇◇◇◇◇◇◇◇◇◇◇◇◇◇◇◇◇◇◇◇◇◇

517   ON NIKON'S NOSE

Look, I spy Nikon's hooked nose, Menippos,
and the face itself cannot be far removed.
Be patient, friend, and let us wait,
for it stands no more than half a mile behind:
the parabolic snout leads the way
and if we climb a high hill
    we may catch a glimpse of the face.

518   A PHYSICIAN'S TOUCH

Only yesterday the good Dr. Markos
laid his sure hand on a statue of Zeus.
Although he was Zeus and made of marble
               we're burying him today.

519   MISTAKEN IDENTITY

Your mouth and your ass, Theodoros,
smell so alike, only the supple mind
of men of science can tell them apart.
Really, you should label your mouth and your ass,
for when you speak I think you are farting.

520 KISSING*

If you kiss me you hate me; if you hate me
    you kiss me,
but if you don't hate me, my sweet friend,
                  don't kiss me.

521 ENIGMA

Who knows when Diodoros is yawning or farting?
For above and below, his breath is the same.

522 POPULAR SINGER AND A BIRD'S DEATH

Deadly is the singing of the night-raven,
but when you, Demophilos, break into song,
even the night-raven croaks.

523 BIG WOMEN

A plump woman with beautiful limbs
    is always good:
whether she is just ripe or very old.
If young, she takes me in her arms
                and hugs.
If old and wrinkled, she licks.

* *Kiss* also means here *copulate*.

[219]

Lucillius

*Epigrammatist of the middle of
the first century* A.D. *He was expert
at the sharply pointed joke and
lampoon; Nero was his patron.*

◇◇◇◇◇◇◇◇◇◇◇◇◇◇◇◇◇◇◇◇◇◇◇◇◇◇◇◇◇

524   SHOPPING TIP
Lady, you went to the market
and picked up hair, rouge, honey, wax and teeth.

For a like amount
                    you might have bought a face.

525   GOSSIP
Some have passed the word you dye your hair.
They lie, Nikilla,
for in the open market
                    you bought it raven black.

526   ON THE HARD LUCK OF DIOPHON
Diophon was being crucified,
but when he saw another near him on a higher
    cross,
he died of envy.

527   LOVE OF LEARNING
Zenonis gives a place in her home to Menandros
                    a bearded grammarian,
for she has delivered her son to his instruction;
and the bushy pedant even labors into night,
                    with the mother,

[220]

practicing their figures, her dangling participles
and his copulative verb.

528   A MONEYLOVER
When miserly Kriton wants to ease his cramping
    stomach
he sniffs not mint
but a copper penny.

529   ON HERMON THE MISER
After spending some money in his sleep,
Hermon the miser was so hopping mad,

he hanged himself.

530   CONTAGION
Demostratis walks in a halo
                    of armpit aroma,
but worse,
she makes those who smell her
        exhale the same he-goat fumes.

531   A NIGHT CALL
Diophantos went to bed and dreamed of
                    Dr. Hermogenes,
and though he was wearing a good-luck piece,
                    he never woke up.

532   ON THE SAME HERMOGENES
The barber is perplexed.
Where can he start to shave the head
of this hairy Hermogenes
who—from head to toe—
seems to be all head?

533   EPITAPH OF A PUGILIST
We his grateful opponents erected this statue
      To Apis a Thoughtful Boxer
who even when clinching never hurt any of us.

534   ON BOXERS
Here you see the ruins of a former Olympic star.
Once he had a real nose, mind you, a chin, forehead,
      ears, and eyes (lids and all),
and then he went pro.

He scrambled everything,
even his share of his father's estate.
For his kid brother showed up
(a spitting image of the former champ)
and the pug
(who looked like an outsider now)
was quietly but sternly ushered away.

535   THE DEVOUT BOXER
Aulos the boxer dedicates his skull to the Lord
      of Pisa,*
having collected the bones one by one.
If he comes out alive from his match at Nemea,
he may, Lord Zeus,
honor you with any surviving ribs.

536   A PRECAUTION
Lazy Markos dreamt he was running, running,
      running. . . .
Out of fear he might run again
Markos never went back to bed.

* Lord of Pisa: Zeus.

[222]

537 THE QUEST

We were searching for the giant Eumekios.
We found him sleeping with his arms outstretched,

all under a tiny saucer.

538 A PROSTITUTE BATHING

A girl of a hundred and still in the *métier*,
Heliodora, you spend hours in the bath.
But I know your dream: you pray to grow young,
like old Pelias, by letting them boil you alive.

539 INSIDE AN ATOM

So skinny was the pin-head Markos
that he bore a hole
                        with his own skull
through an atom of Epikouros
                        and slipped inside.

540 FIDELITY IN THE ARTS

Eutychos the portrait painter got twenty sons,
but even among his children—never one likeness.

541 THE POET DESCENDING

Eutychides the lyric poet is dead.
Escape! you who inhabit the underworld,
for he comes with odes,
and orders thirteen lyres and twenty crates of music
to burn beside him on his funeral pyre.
Now Charon has you,
for where can you escape
with Eutychides established in Hell?

542   DECORUM

The miser Asklepiades finding a mouse
one evening in his house, saluted it:
"My very dear mouse, what do you want
    from me?"
With its sweetest smile the mouse replied:
"My dear friend and ceremonious host,
put away your fears,
I did not come for board—merely a bed."

Leonidas of Alexandria

Wrote between A.D. 55 and 85.
Nero and later emperors were his
patrons. More than forty of his
epigrams are in the Anthology.
Thirty are composed in such a way
that the letters of each couplet in
a poem, if given a numerical
value, produce the same total.

543   THE PUNISHMENT
The grape-stealer Hekatonymos
            ran all the way down to Hades
                    flogged with a stolen vine switch.

Traianus (The Emperor Trajan)

*Lived from A.D. 53 to 117. He was
one of the best of Rome's emperors. For the ruling classes at
Rome, Greek was, like French in
modern times, a mark of one's
sophistication.*

✧✧✧✧✧✧✧✧✧✧✧✧✧✧✧✧✧✧✧✧✧✧✧✧✧✧✧✧✧✧

544   A NATURAL SUNDIAL

If you point your b i g nose sunward
and open your gaping
                              mouth,
                                        all who pass by
will know the time of day.

Ammianus

*Lived at the beginning of the
second century* A.D.

✧✧✧✧✧✧✧✧✧✧✧✧✧✧✧✧✧✧✧✧✧✧✧✧✧✧✧✧✧✧

545   ON THE AFTERLIFE OF NEARCHOS
May the dust lie lightly on you in your grave,
O wretched Nearchos,
that wild dogs may more easily drag you out.

Loukianos (Lucian)

Born about A.D. *120 in Samosata in Syria; died sometime after 180. An itinerant teacher of rhetoric and Cynic philosophy, he was also the author of numerous satirical dialogues and other writings, including the fabulous* True History, *which influenced (among others) Rabelais and Swift.*

546   ON MAGICAL WHISKERS

If by growing a goatee you hope to come
    upon wisdom,
then, O wise friend, any smelly goat in
                a handsome beard
is at once Plato.

Dionysius Sophistes

One of many poets, sophists, philosophers and miscellaneous writers of the same name who lived in the Roman period.

547   A VENDOR OF FLOWERS
You selling roses have a flowery charm.
But rose-girl, what are you selling me?
              your roses? yourself? or both?

Julianus (Julian the Apostate)

A.D. 332-363. The Roman emperor who, among his other reforms, tried belatedly to stem the tide of Christianity and revitalize paganism. He wrote numerous prose works in Greek.

548   CALCULATION*

Konon is but two feet tall—his wife four.
When flat in bed
            their feet touching the wall,
imagine where Konon keeps his lips.

* Attribution to Julianus is uncertain.

Aisopos

Ca. fourth century A.D. *(Not the semilegendary fabulist of a thousand years earlier.)*

549   FUTILITY

How can we escape from you, life, except through
   death?
Our sorrows are endless. Endure? Escape? Neither
   is easy.
Yes, the beauty of nature is sweet—the earth,
       sea, stars,
             the orbit of the moon and sun.
But all else is fear and pain.
One day a bit of luck
and then we wait for inexorable Nemesis.

The
Byzantine Period

Sarah Tzalos Barnstone

Palladas

Active about A.D. *400. An impoverished schoolmaster at Alexandria,
a pagan among Christians, he
wrote more than 150 epigrams,
most of them hopeless and bitter.*

◇◇◇◇◇◇◇◇◇◇◇◇◇◇◇◇◇◇◇◇◇◇◇◇◇◇◇◇◇◇◇

550   HER GLORIOUS HOUR
A woman will gnaw at your bile
Yet she has two fine seasons:
        one, in her bridal bed;
        two, when she is dead.*

551   HERITAGE
A grammarian's daughter made love with a man,
and the poor creature gave birth to a child
who was, in orderly sequence:
        masculine, feminine, & neuter.

552   ON THE RHETOR MAUROS
I was thunderstruck
on beholding Mauros, Professor of Rhetoric,
raise his elephantine snout
and spew murder in a voice
made from lips weighing one pound apiece.

553   ON MONKS
If solitary, how can they be so many?
If many, how again are they solitary?
O crowd of solitaries feigning solitude!

* Occasionally, in Greek, such an example of internal rhyme as *thalamo*
and *thanato* is used, especially for humor and satire.

554 THE SLAUGHTERHOUSE
We all are watched over and foddered for death
   like a herd of pigs absurdly butchered.

555 A PAGAN IN ALEXANDRIA CONSIDERS
LIFE UNDER CHRISTIAN MOBS WHO
ARE DESTROYING ANTIQUITY
Is it true that we Greeks are really dead
and only seem alive—in our fallen state
where we imagine that a dream is life?
Or are we truly alive and is life dead?

556 GRAVE WARNING
Sir, you talk a lot, and after a short span
   are laid out in the earth.
Keep silent
and while you are alive, meditate on death.

Julianus (Julian the Prefect of Egypt)

Active during the sixth century A.D.

◇◇◇◇◇◇◇◇◇◇◇◇◇◇◇◇◇◇◇◇◇◇◇◇◇◇◇◇◇◇

557   ON A YOUNG WIFE
O black winter of savage death
that froze the spring of your unnumbered charms.
The tomb tore you from brilliant day
in this, your bitter sixteenth year.
Your husband and father—blind with grief—
Think of you, Anastasia, who were our sun.

558   GIFT FROM THE DEAD
Your dear husband, Rhodo, erects a monument
of shining marble to redeem your soul;
he gives money to the poor—for, kindest of wives,
you died early and gladdened him with
freedom.

559   AT ANAKREON'S TOMB
I often sang this, and even from the grave I shout:
drink, for soon you must put on this garment of
dust.

560   ON ANAKREON
A. You died from filling your paunch with wine,
Anakreon.
B. But I enjoyed it, and you who do not drink will
also find yourself in Hades.

Paulus Silentiarius

An official at the court of Justinian ca. A.D. 560. He wrote about eighty epigrams in the Anthology, *including some of the liveliest love poems.*

561   VISIONS
A man bitten by a mad hound, they say,
sees an image of the beast in the water.

Is Eros then wild with rabies?
Did he gash me with his bitter tooth
and ravage my spirit with his heat?

For now I see your darling form mirrored
in winecup, river whirlpool and the sea.

562   TABOO
My fingers on her breasts, our mouths joined;
I graze with deep fury on her silver neck;
yet though I labor over Aphrogeneia
this virgin lets me go so far—and denies
me her bed.
            Her upper body she allows
to Aphrodite, but her under parts she commits
to chaste Athena. I waste away between.

563   PURITY
Beautiful girl, let us cast off these garments.
Let our naked limbs be knotted
so that no space is left between.

To me the clothes you wear are as strong
as the great wall of Babylon.*
Let us press chest against chest,
mouth into mouth,
and plunge the rest into silence.
I cannot bear trivial chatter.

* Wall erected by Semiramis.

Agathias Scholastikos

Lived from A.D. *536 to 582. He was
a lawyer of Byzantium, and com-
piler of the epigram-anthology
which was the basis for the existing* Greek Anthology. *Agathias
was a friend of Paulus Silentiarius
but not his poetic equal.*

564   INTIMATE DIALOG

A. What are you mooning about?

B. I am in love.

A. With whom?

B. A virgin.

A. Is she good looking?

B. Perfectly exquisite.

A. Where did you meet her?

B. At a dinner party. I found her lying on the same
couch with me.

A. You think you'll get in?

B. Yes, yes, my friend, but I don't wish to broad-
cast it. Actually I want it to be nice and discreet.

A. You mean you want to avoid marriage.

B. My friend, I found out she isn't worth a dime.

A. You know this already. You are not in love,
dear friend. You are lying. How can your heart
be madly in love when it calculates so well?

Damaskios

Ca. fifth-sixth centuries A.D.

◇◇◇◇◇◇◇◇◇◇◇◇◇◇◇◇◇◇◇◇◇◇◇◇◇◇◇◇◇◇◇

565   EPITAPH OF A SLAVE GIRL
Zozime, you were a slave girl only in body
and now find freedom for your body too.

Julianus (Julian Antecessor)

Sixth century A.D.*?*

❖❖❖❖❖❖❖❖❖❖❖❖❖❖❖❖❖❖❖❖❖❖❖❖❖❖❖

566   WINNING CHARM
Your face is the face of an ostrich.

Was it Circe in her island sanctuary
who made you drink her secret potion
to turn your sourpuss into a birdhead?

567   HARVESTING
Tall and wavy are the crops
                       on your hairy face.
Scissors?
          Never.
Throw them away and bring out a plow.

Authors and Anonymous
Works of Indefinite Period

Glykon

Little is known of Glykon. He is credited by Hephaistion with the invention of the Glykonic meter, but the Glykon of the Greek Anthology, *where this single poem appears under that name, may be a later poet of the same name.*

568   LIFE WITHOUT MEANING

All is laughter and dust. And all is nothing,
   since out of unreason comes all that is.

Kallikteros

A poet known only through his poems in the Palatine Anthology.

✦✦✦✦✦✦✦✦✦✦✦✦✦✦✦✦✦✦✦✦✦✦✦✦✦✦

569   A SKILLFUL THIEF
Rhodo removes leprosy and scrofula by drugs
    and removes the rest with agile fingers.

570   BARTERED VIRTUE
The unpurchased wheat in your home may inform
    you
    that your dear wife has been a horn of plenty.

Ammonides

Known only through the Palatine Anthology.

❖❖❖❖❖❖❖❖❖❖❖❖❖❖❖❖❖❖❖❖❖❖❖❖❖❖❖❖❖❖

571   A WAR PLAN

Show off Antipatra naked to the Parthians,
and the enemy will flee beyond the horizon,
yes, beyond the pillars of Herakles.

Diophanes of Myrina

Known only through the Palatine Anthology.

572   FOR A STATUE OF EROS

Love is really a highway robber:
1) He waits in ambush through the night,
2) He is a desperado,
3) and in the end he strips us naked.

The Anakreonteia

These imitations, long attributed to Anakreon, were written between the first century B.C. *and the sixth century* A.D.

◇◇◇◇◇◇◇◇◇◇◇◇◇◇◇◇◇◇◇◇◇◇◇◇◇◇◇◇◇◇◇◇◇◇

573   THE OLD MAN

Anakreon, singer of Teos,
came to me in a dream
and laughingly called me.
And I ran up to him
and kissed and hugged him.
He was old but handsome
and wild over wine.
His lips smelled of grape.
Though old and tottery
he fed on love. He slipped
the wreath from his head
and offered it to me.
It smelled of Anakreon.
I stupidly took it
and stuck it in my hair,
and ever since, I can't
keep myself from loving.

574   THE WELL-TEMPERED PARTY

Bring Homer's lyre but mute
the chords of savage war.
Bring winecups and the laws
of proper revelry.
I shall get drunk and dance
at our party, and even
roar on my tanging lyre,

yet with a tempered fury.
Bring Homer's lyre but mute
the chords of savage war.

575   THE RUB OF LOVE
        Once while plaiting a wreath
        I found Eros among the roses.
        I grabbed him by the wings
        and dipped him in the wine
        and drank him down.
        Now inside my limbs
        he tickles me with his wings.

576   PLAY BEFORE DEATH
        "Anakreon, you are old,"
        the women say to me.
        "Look in the mirror, you
        haven't one lonely patch
        on your abandoned temples
        or desolate pate." Yes,
        I cannot boast about
        my hair, but I know this:
        an old man must have love
        the closer he is to death.

577   TODAY
        I don't care for Gyges' gold,
        the king of fabled Sardis,
        for money is repugnant.
        I don't envy the despots.
        I live to soak my beard
        in perfume, and twine my hair
        in roses. Day is my gold.
        Who can tell the future?
        So while sun is sweet, drink,
        shoot dice and offer a toast
        to Bakchos. Tomorrow
        disease may cut your wine.

578   A NUISANCE

What can I do to you,
verbose swallow? Shall I
clip your agile wings
or slit your sharp tongue
like a heartless Tereus?
Why do your morning cries
rip me from my dreams
of my tender Bathyllos?

579   BARGAIN

A young peddler was hawking
a wax replica of Eros.
I went to him and said:
"How much is the statue?"
He answered me in Doric.
"You name it. Just so
I can get rid of him.
I'm no sculptor in wax
and I am sick of living
with this grubby Eros."
Now Eros, make me burn
or I'll melt you in fire.

580   ARITHMETIC

If you can count the leaves
of trees, waves in the ocean,
I shall make you the sole
accountant of my loves.
Mark down 20 from Athens,
and throw in 15 more.
From Corinth a small army
(Greek women are splendid!)
From Lesbos and Ionia,
Karia and Rhodes: 2,000
satisfying affairs.
Do my numbers overwhelm you?
I haven't mentioned Syria

[251]

or love in Egypt and Krete
where in the cities love
is both refined and wild.
And shall I count up those
from Cadiz and from far
Afghanistan and India?

581   A WOMAN

Nature gave the bull horns
and nimble hooves to horses,
springing legs to the hare,
a chasm of teeth to lions.
She furnished fins to fish
and speckled wings to birds.
To man she offered wisdom.
Was nothing left for woman?
Yes, she gave her beauty
in place of shields and swords,
and beauty glides in victory
over virile swords and fire.

582   STRATAGEM

You chant of Theban battles
or the slaughter before Troy.
I tell of my disaster,
It was no horse or hoplite,
no black vessel in the port.
A new weapon hobbled me:
two eyes stuck me to the bone.

583   THE TEST

Eros came and struck me
with his hyacinth rod
and ordered me to come.
We crossed uncrossable
torrents; forests, cliffs.
We raced, dripping sweat:
my heart was in my mouth,

my body nearly dead.
Then Eros touched my forehead
with his deft wing, and spoke:
"Are you unable to love?"

584   BEFORE THE SHADOWS
Lying on a soft bed
of myrtle and lotus
I want to drink.
Eros, put your apron on
with the papyrus ribbon,
and pour my dark wine.
Like a swift wheel
our life speeds past
and soon we will lie:
dust of scattered bones.
Why waste those perfumes
on the soil by my grave?
While I live, bring flowers
and my lovely mistress.
Before my somber climb
down to death's choir,
I would forget my grief.

585   THE MIDNIGHT GUEST
Once in the frozen hours of night
While the Great Bear circled Arktouros
and mortals lay drugged with sleep,
Eros stood at my gate, knocking.
"Who is pounding on my door?" I said.
"You are splitting my dreams."
"Open up. I'm only a child.
Don't be alarmed," Eros called in.
"I'm dripping wet and lost
and the night is black and moonless."
Hearing his words I pitied him
and quickly lit a candle.
Opening a door I saw a boy

with bow, wings and quiver.
I sat him down by the fire
and warmed his hands with my own,
and squeezed water from his hair.
When he recovered from the cold
he said, "Let's test this bow.
Rain has weakened the string."
He drew and struck me square
in the groin like a gadfly.
He leapt up laughing with scorn:
"Stranger, let us be happy.
My bow is unharmed, but you
will have trouble in your heart."

586   CICADA

We bless you, cicada,
high in the branches.
You sip a dew drop
and whistle like a king.
What you see is yours:
all the soft meadows
and furry mountains.
Yet you do no harm
in the farmer's field,
and men exalt you
as the voice of summer.
You are loved by Muses
and Apollo himself
who gave you clear song.
Wise child of the earth,
old age doesn't waste you.
Unfeeling and bloodless
you are like a god.

587   GOLD, DEATH, WINE

If gold could buy life,
I would guard my wealth
with jealous desire,

and when death came
he would take some
and leave me alone.
Yet being mortal
I cannot prolong
my life, so why
should I cry or moan?
If we must die,
what good is gold?
So bring sweet wine,
and when I've drunk
bring my good friends.
I'll lie on a soft bed
and be lost in love.

588   REFLECTION

How good it is to roam
on the ripe grassy meadows
where the sweet wind drifts;
look at the grapevines,
and lie under the leaves
with a soft girl in my arms
who is willing and warm.

589   SPRING

Spring comes: see where
Graces leave the rose,
how the ruffled sea
smooths into peace,
the water-duck dives,
how the crane soars.
The hot sun burns up
the somber clouds;
fields shine with crops
and olive trees bud.
Everywhere the flood
of swollen grapes
flowers in the vineyard.

590   ADAPTABILITY

Once the daughter of Tantalos*
became a stone on the Phrygian hills,
and the daughter of Pandion
flew into the sky as a swallow.
I wish I were a mirror
so you would look at me.
I wish I were a tunic
so you would always wear me.
I should like to be water
so I could bathe your body.
I would become myrrh
so I could anoint you.
I would gladly be a scarf
for your breasts, a pearl
for your throat, a sandal—
if you would be sure to step on me.

591   DRUNKARD

The black earth drinks
and trees suck rain.
The seas drink brooks
and sun the sea
and moon the sun.
Why do you rage, friends,
when I want to drink?

* The daughter of Tantalos was Niobe.

Miscellaneous

592   ON A DROWNED SAILOR

Do not ask, mariner, whose tomb I am,
but chance your life upon a kinder sea.

593   PLEASURE*

To praise is the highest good, and censure
is the beginning of hatred,
yet to speak maliciously of one's neighbor
is, after all, Attic honey.

594   A BITTER TALE

After eating little and drinking less,
I suffered the pains of lingering disease.
I have lived long and now am dead. I say:
a curse on you all!

595   METAMORPHOSIS

I wish I were a scarlet rose
so you might lift me in your hands
and pull me to your snowy breasts.

596   BY THE SEA

If I were the wind
you might walk slowly along the shore
and remove your dress
and, as I blow, take me to your naked breasts.

* Sometimes attributed to Palladas.

597   A PRIVATE BATH

Delicious girl of the bath,
why do you rub so fiercely
                    when you bathe me?
Before I am fully undressed
I feel the fire.

598   PRAYER TO APHRODITE

Kypris, if you save those from the pelagos,
save me: I founder shipwrecked on the land.

599   DREAMS

Sthenelais (who is an expensive whore and burns
              up the town, breathing a smell of gold
                    on all those who desire her)
lay naked with me and came and came
                    through my dreamy night,
all for nothing until the pleasant dawn.

Nor more will I crawl before that barbarous girl
nor sink into the sticky juice of self-pity,
for sleep gives me gratuit
                    my fill of sweet flesh.

600   ON GORGIOS

I am the head of the Cynic Gorgios—
no longer spitting or blowing my nose.

601   FOREST MUSIC*

Come, sit under my pine tree which is shaking
pleasantly as it plays with the mild west wind,
and hear the gossipy riverlets where I finger
my lonely reeds—and merge into soft sleep.

* Similar to a poem ascribed to Plato, 454 B.C.

602 HIS PATIENCE

You denied me your green grape.
When ripe, you sent me on my way.
Do you now begrudge me
a small bite of your dry raisin?

603 PROKLOS

Proklos cannot wipe his nose with his hand,
his arms being shorter than the wild snout,
and when the poor thing sneezes, he won't even
say,
    Zeus preserve us!
            He cannot hear his nose,
his ears being O so far away.

604 AT THE TOMB OF ANAKREON

Stranger, passing near the tomb of Anakreon,
pour me a libation as you approach,
for in life I was a drunkard.

605 ON PLATO'S TOMB

Apollo had two sons, Asklepios and Plato:
one to save the body; the other the soul.

606 EPITAPH OF THE PHILOSOPHER EPIKTETOS

I was a slave: crippled in body and poor
as the beggar Iros—yet loved by the gods.

607 HER UNIQUE VIRTUE

Under this slab I rest, famous among women,
    having opened my legs for one man alone.

608 ON DIONYSIOS OF TARSOS

At sixty I, Dionysios, lie in my grave.
I was from Tarsos,
I never married and wish my father had not.

[259]

609   THE EXPECTATION

I no longer mourn those gone from the sweet light
   but those who live ever waiting for death.

610   BREVITY

The rose blooms for a brief season. It fades,
and when one looks again—the rose is briar.

Folksongs

❖❖❖❖❖❖❖❖❖❖❖❖❖❖❖❖❖❖❖❖❖❖❖❖❖❖❖❖

611   THE OWL

Send the screaming owl of night
away from our land, away
from our people. Send
the contemptible bird
to our enemy's fleet of quick ships.

612   AGING LOVER'S APPEAL*

Please—keep old age
away a while longer,
O beautiful Aphrodite.

613   DAWN

What happened to you? Don't betray me,
I beg you.
Before he comes, get up from the bed
so you won't hurt yourself or me.
I am unhappy!
It is already day.
Don't you see the light in the window?

614   THE SUN

Shine on us,
friendly sun.

* Diehl attributes this song to Alkman.

Glossary
and Index

✦✦✦✦✦✦✦✦✦✦✦✦✦✦✦✦✦✦✦✦✦✦✦✦✦✦✦✦✦✦✦✦✦

"In." followed by poet's name refers to the headnotes on the
poet; "Te." followed by poet's name refers to testimonia on the
poet; numbers refer to poems in which the cited word occurs.

[263]

Agido—Proper name. 72

Aiakos—Son of Zeus, father of Peleus and grandfather of Achilles, he was known as a just man and a judge in the underworld. 106

Aietes—King of Kolchis and father of Medeia. 278

Aigaian (Aegean) Sea—That part of the Mediterranean Sea between Greece and Asia Minor. 2, 457, 515

Aigialos—A city of Amorgos founded by the poet Simonides. Te. Simonides

Aigisthos (Aegisthus)—Surviving son of Thyestes and lover of Agamemnon's wife, Klytaimnestra. 289

Ainesidamos—Father of Theron. 426

Ainesimbrota—Proper name. 72

Ainos—Aiolic city at mouth of Hebros River. 105

Aiolic/Aiolia—Dialect of eastern Greece (Aiolia) in which Sappho and Alkaios wrote. In. Alkman, In. Alkaios, In. Sappho, 283, 390, In. Theokritos

Aiolos—Father of Sisyphos. 119

Aischylides—Proper name. 43

Aischylos (Aeschylus)—Greek tragic poet generally regarded as the founder of Greek tragedy. In. Simonides

Aisimides—Proper name. 41

Aithra—Daughter of Pittheus, King of Troizen, and mother of Theseus. 431

Aitolia—A division of Greece celebrated in mythology as the home of the Kalydonian boar hunt. 426

Akragas (Agrigentum)—A city on the southern coast of Sicily known for its splendor. In. Stesichoros, In. Simonides, In. Pindaros, 426

Alexandria/Alexandrian—The capital of Egypt, founded by Alexander the Great, and the center of learning and culture during the Hellenistic period. The Library of Alexandria is said to have contained over half a million volumes. In. Mimnermos, In. Stesichoros, In. Kallimachos, In. Theokritos, In. Asklepiades, In. Nikarchos, In. Palladas, 555

Alexis—Proper name. 447

Alkaios—Lyric poet of Mytilene of Lesbos (fl. ca. 611-580 B.C.). In. Alkaios, In. Terpandros, 107, In. Sappho, Te. Sappho, 201, In. Ibykos, Te. Ibykos, 245, 257, In. Anakreon, Te. Bakchylides, In. Theokritos

Alkestis (Alcestis)—Daughter of Pelias and wife of Admetos. 291

Alkibia—Proper name. 33

Alkman—Lyric poet of the second half of the seventh century B.C. His work is concerned mainly with Spartan feasts and festivals. In. Alkman, In. Terpandros, 67, 77, 79, In. Stesichoros, Te. Bakchylides, 612

Alkmena—Daughter of Elektryon, King of Mykenai, and wife of Amphitryon. Mother of Herakles by Zeus. 378

Alpheus—One of the largest rivers in Greece. As a hunter, Alpheus pursued the nymph Arethosia; he was transformed into a river, she into a spring. See *Arethosia*. 415, 426

Ammianus Marcellinus—Last of the great Roman historians, he wrote a history of the Roman Empire from A.D. 353 to 378. Te. Stesichoros

Amorgos—An island of the Aigaian Sea and the birthplace of Simonides. In. Simonides, Te. Simonides, 209

Amphiptolemos—Father of Asios. Te. Asios

Amphitrite—Daughter of Nereus and wife of Poseidon. 431

Amphitryon—Son of Alkaios, grandson of Perseus and husband of Alkmena. Amphitryon's son refers to Herakles. 426, 429

Amyklian—Of Amyklai, an ancient town in Lakonia. 420

Anakreon—Lyric poet of Teos (ca. 560 B.C.). In. Anakreon, In. Ibykos, Te. Ibykos, In. Simonides, Te. Hipparchos, Te. Bakchylides, In. Anakreonteia, 559, 560, 572, 576, 604

Anaktoria—One of Sappho's friends. One theory is that she left Sappho in order to marry a soldier stationed in Sardis. In. Sappho, 124, 141

Anastasia—Proper name. 557

Anatolia—The peninsula of Asia Minor. In. Mimnermos

Andromache—Daughter of Eetion, King of Thebes, and wife of Hektor. Her husband was killed by Achilles during the Trojan War, her son Astyanax was put to death, and she herself was taken prisoner by the Greeks. 187

Andromeda—A rival of Sappho, perhaps a poet. In. Sappho, 144, 190, 191, 192, 259

Andros—The most northerly island of the Kyklades. 515, In. Sappho

Anthology—See PALATINE ANTHOLOGY. In. Philodemos, In. Diodoros, In. Antipatros of Thessalonike, In. Nikarchos, In. Leonidas, In. Paulus Silentiarius

Antigone—Proper name. 510

Antimenidas—Brother of the poet Alkaios, who fought with the Babylonian army under Nebuchadnezzar in the early 6th century B.C. 101

Antipatros of Sidon—Greek epigrammatist who influenced Catullus and other Republican poets (fl. 1st century B.C.). Te. Pindaros

Antipatros of Thessalonike—Greek epigrammatist of the

Aristarchos—Grammarian and great critic of antiquity. The founder of scientific scholarship. Te. Archilochos

Aristodemos—Pupil of Sokrates, one of the Seven Sages. 104, Te. Melanippides

Aristogeiton—Assassin, along with Harmodios, of the tyrant Hipparchos in 511 B.C. In. Hipparchos, Te. Hipparchos

Aristophanes—Greatest playwright of comedy in antiquity (ca. 450-ca. 385 B.C.). 456

Aristophon—Proper name. 46

Aristotle—Great Greek philosopher (384-322 B.C.). Te. Solon, Te. Xenophanes, Te. Simonides, Te. Hipparchos, Te. Hippon, Te. Timotheos, 376

Aristoxenos—Philosopher and musician (fl. ca. 318 B.C.). Te. Lamprokles

Arkadia—A country in the middle of the Peloponnesos. The Arkadians regarded themselves as the most ancient people of Greece. 426, In. Anyte

Arkesime—A city of Amorgos founded by Simonides. Te. Simonides

Arktouros—A bright star near the constellation of the Great Bear. 585

Artemis—The twin sister of Apollo, daughter of Zeus and Leto. She was the goddess of chastity, the hunt, the moon and childbirth. 88, 245, 318, 415, 512.

Artemis Orthosia—Artemis was frequently identified with the Dorian goddess, Orthia, who was worshiped at Sparta as Artemis Orthosia. 426

Artemon—Proper name. 329

Asimides—Proper name. 41

Asklepiades—Proper name. 542

Asklepias—Proper name. 495

Asklepios—The god of the art of medicine. The son of Apollo and the pupil of Chiron, Asklepios was killed by Zeus because he could raise the dead. Te. Platon. 605

Astaphis—Proper name. 72

Astypalaia—Sister of Europa. Te. Asios

Athena (Athene, Pallas)—Goddess of wisdom, war, arts and sciences. The daughter of Zeus. 10, In. Stesichoros, 280, 337, 418, 429, 431, 562

Athenaios—Greek grammarian (ca. A.D. 230). Te. Tyrtaios, Te. Asios, Te. Timokreon

Athenis—A Chian sculptor satirized by Hipponax.

Athens—The capital of Attica. In. Tyrtaios, In. Hipponax, Te. Tyrtaios, In. Solon, 261, In. Anakreon, In. Simonides, Te. Apollodoros, In. Hipparchos, Te. Hippa, In. Lamprokles,

Charon—The boatman who ferried the dead across the rivers of the underworld. Also means "underworld." 541

Charon—Proper name. 31

Charybdis—A giant whirlpool opposite the cave of Skylla off the coast of Sicily. 314, 490

Cheiron—The wisest of the Centaurs, known for his skills in medicine, music, art, hunting and gymnastics. He was accidentally killed by Herakles and later placed among the stars as Sagittarius. 106

Chian/Chios (Scio)—Of Chios, a large island south of Lesbos, near Asia Minor. Celebrated for its wine and marble, Chios was reputed to be the birthplace of Homer. 63, 142, 317, Te. Pindaros, Te. Theokritos

Chrysilla—Proper name.

Cicero—Great Roman orator, statesman and essayist (106-43 B.C.). Te. Ibykos, Te. Anakreon

Cimmerian incursions—Invasions of Assyria and Asia Minor in the eighth and seventh centuries B.C. by barbarians from southern Russia. In. Kallinos, 55

Circe—A beautiful witch famous for her magical powers, who held Odysseus captive on her island. Daughter of the sun-god Helios. 566

Clement of Alexandria—One of the early Greek Fathers, important because of his extensive knowledge of Greek literature and philosophy (ca. A.D. 160-215). In. Archilochos

Cupid—See Eros. In. Asklepiades

Cynic—Member of a school of philosophy founded at Athens by Antisthenes, pupil of Sokrates. The name is taken from the Kynosarges gymnasium where the school was established. In. Meleagros, In. Loukianos

Daidalos—Legendary Athenian craftsman who with his son Ikaros escaped from their prison tower with wings made of wax and feathers. Ikaros flew too near the sun and fell into the sea, hence the name Ikarian Sea. Te. Pindaros

Damareta—Proper name. 72

Damon of Athens—Celebrated musician and Sophist, teacher of Perikles and Sokrates. Te. Lamprokles

Danaë—A girl of Argos, whose father prophesied that her son would kill him. To prevent the conception of a son her father enclosed her in a chamber. Zeus penetrated the chamber in a shower of gold and begot Perseus. 374, 482, 516

Danaids—The daughters of Danaos. 439

Glossary and Index

Daphnis—A Sicilian shepherd, son of Hermes and regarded as the inventor of bucolic poetry. 471, 472, 473

Darius—King of Persia (521-485 B.C.). During his reign the great war between the Persians and the Greeks began. 464

Deianeira—Wife of Herakles. 429

Delos—The center island of the Kyklades in the Aigaian Sea. The birthplace of Apollo and Artemis and an important center for their worship. 431

Delphi—An ancient oracular shrine of Apollo in Phokis, and also a center for theatrical and athletic events. 107, 370, Te. Hipparchos, 429, 474

Demeter—Daughter of Kronos and Rhea and the mother of Persephone. She was the goddess of corn and a patroness of agriculture. 390

Demophilos—Proper name. 522

Demos—Proper name. 487

Demostratis—Proper name. 530

Denthiades—A town of Lakonia. 82

Diagorases—Famous boxer of Rhodes praised in Pindar's Olympic Ode VII. 421

Diagoras—Poet and philosopher, known for his atheism. Te. Xenophanes

Didyme—Proper name. 480

Didymos—Of Alexandria, nicknamed "brazen-guts" because of his great industry. This author of the first century B.C. wrote a commentary on Homer. Te. Anakreon

Dika—Probably short for MNASIDIKA, one of Sappho's friends. 214

Diodoros—Poet of the *Greek Anthology*. In. Diodoros, 506

Diodoros—Proper name. 527

Diogenes—Proper name. 515

Diogenes—A cynical philosopher (ca. 400 B.C.) known in Athens for his pithy sayings. Te. Ibykos

Diogenes Laertios—Author of *Lives and Opinions of Eminent Philosophers*, an account of the principal Greek thinkers of his day (fl. A.D. 150). Te. Solon, Te. Xenophanes, Te. Platon

Diokleia—Proper name. 509

Dion—Son of Hipparinos and son-in-law of the Syracusian tyrant Dionysios the Elder, Dion was a disciple of Plato and a statesman in Sicily. 461

Dionysios—Proper name. 608

Dionysos (Bakchos)—Greek god of wine and fertility. The son of Zeus and Semele, Dionysos was the god of natural vitality also. 149, 344, 499

Diophantos—Proper name. 531

Dioskouri—From the Greek "Dios Kouri," literally "sons of Zeus," or Kastor and Polydeukes. These twin sons of Zeus and Leda were regarded as both courageous gods and mortals and were later identified with the constellation Gemini. 75, 95, 426

Diphilos—Proper name. 515

Dirphian/Dirphys. Central mountain range of Euboia. 362

Doric/Dorian—Dialect of Greek used in Sparta. In. Alkman, In. Stesichoros, In. Ibykos, In. Simonides, 426, In. Bakchylides, In. Anyte, In. Melanippides, In. Theokritos, Te. Bion

Dodekanese—Twelve islands in the southeast Aigaian Sea. In. Theokritos

Doricha—Egyptian courtesan and lover of Sappho's brother, Charaxos. 235

Dotian Plain—Part of Pelasgiotis in Thessaly. 420

Dryads—(Hamadryads). The nymphs of the trees. 455

Ekbatana—The capital of Media, a country of Asia above Persia. 457

Elea—A town on the west coast of Lakonia. Here Parmenides founded the Eleatic school of philosophy. In. Xenophanes

Elis—A state in the northwest of the Peloponnesos, which included the important site of Olympia. Te. Bakchylides

Elpiniki—Proper name. 48

Elpis—Proper name. 512

Elysium—In mythology, the residence of the blessed after death. 422

Emmenos—Children of Emmenos refers to the family of Theron. 426

Empedokles—Philosopher and scientist of Akragas (fl. ca. 460 B.C.). The inventor of the art of rhetoric. Te. Theognis

Enyalios—Epithet of the god Ares and later a different god of war. 25

Ephesos—One of the principal Ionian cities on the coast of Asia Minor. In. Kallinos, Te. Kallinos, In. Hipponax, In. Xenophanes, 512

Epikouros (Epicurus)—Greek philosopher (341-270 B.C.) and founder of the Epicurean school of philosophy. Te. Xenophanes, 539

Epiktetos—Stoic philosopher of first century A.D. 606

Epinikion—A victory ode, a form used by Pindar, Bakchylides and Simonides. In. Pindaros

Eretria—A town of Euboia situated on the Euripos Strait. It was destroyed by the Persians in 490 B.C. 27, 412, 457, 460

Ergoteles—A political exile from Krete and a victor in the Olympian games; Krete enjoyed a reputation for its runners. 421

Eriboia—Wife of Telamon and mother of Aias (Ajax). 431

Eros (Cupid)—The god of all striving toward union, particularly of sexual love. Usually regarded as the son of Aphrodite. 87, 126, 153, 258, 297, 299, 321, 324, 488, 496, 561, 575, 579, 583

Erysiche—A city of Arkanania, 77

Erytheia—Birthplace of the monster Geryon, slain by Herakles. It was either Cádiz (Gades), the Balearic Islands, or islands off the coast of Epiros. 292

Euboia—The largest island of the Aigaian Sea and near the mainland. 27, 402, 457, 460

Eudemos—Proper name. 428

Euenor—Father and teacher of Parrhasios. Te. Parrhasios

Eukrates—Father of Meleagros. Te. Meleagros, 501

Eumekios—Proper name. 537

Euripides—One of the three great Attic tragedians (480-406 B.C.). In. Timotheos, Te. Timotheos

Euripos—The strait between Euboia and the mainland. 362

Europa—In mythology, Europa was kidnapped by Zeus in the disguise of a bull and carried off to Krete where she became the mother of Minos. Te. Asios, In. Stesichoros

Eurotas—The chief river in Lakonia. 402

Eurymedon—Proper name. 314

Eurymedon—A river in Pamphylia. 360

Euryalos—A young man loved by Ibykos. 302

Eurysteus—King of Argos for whom Herakles performed his twelve labors. 426

Eurytion—The centaur whom Herakles slew. 292

Eustathios—Grammarian and historian of the eleventh century A.D. Te. Apollodoros

Eutychides—Proper name of a poet. 541

Eutychos—Proper name of a portrait painter. 540

Evenos (Euenos)—A river of Aitolia taking its name from Evenos, whose daughter was kidnapped by Marpessa. Evenos, being unable to rescue his daughter, threw himself into the river. 429

Examyes—Proper name. Te. Mimnermos

Five Hills—A town in Lakonia. 82

Gadara—A city in Syria. Te. Meleagros

Galateia—Sea nymph, daughter of Nereus and Doris, and loved by Polyphemos. 503

Geraneia—The mountain range between the territories of Megara and Corinth. 373

Geryon—A monster with three heads and three bodies joined together, living on the island of Erytheia. 293

Giants—The sons of Ge produced from the blood of the mutilated Uranus. Beings of great size with serpent feet, the Giants were eventually destroyed by Herakles and the other gods and were buried beneath volcanoes. 345

Glaukos—Proper name. 6, 32, 377, 378

Gongyla—One of Sappho's intimate friends. 203

Gorgios—Sicilian rhetorician and orator of the fifth century B.C. A leading Sophist, his writings influenced much of Attic prose, especially the writings of Isokrates. 601

Gorgo—A rival of Sappho's; perhaps a poet. In. Sappho, 167

Gorgo—Proper name. 380

Gortyn—An ancient city in Krete famous for two groups of inscriptions about social institutions written on the interior wall of the courthouse. 382

Graces—Goddesses of grace and charm, associated with the Muses. 161, 162, 184, 214, 296, 302, 456, Te. Meleagros, 501, In. Diphilos, In. Agathias Scholastikos, In. Glykon, 589

Greek Anthology—See PALATINE ANTHOLOGY

Gyara—An island of the Kyklades in the Aigaian Sea. 194

Gyges—King of Lydia whose wealth became proverbial. 31, 309, 577

Gyrai—Some rocks off the island of Mykonos. 6

Gyrinno—One of Sappho's companions. 215

Hades—God of the underworld, or sometimes a name for the underworld itself. 109, 258, 259, 265, 295, Te. Hipponax, 479, 543, 560

Hagesichora—Leader of Alkman's chorus of girls. 72

Halikarnassos—Birthplace of Herodotos. This city of Asia Minor stood in the southwestern part of Karia, opposite the island of Keos. 468

Harmodios—Assassin, along with Aristogeiton, of the tyrant Hipparchos in 511 B.C. In. Hipparchos, Te. Hipparchos

Harmony—Daughter of Ares and Aphrodite, the wife of Kadmus. Te. Pindaros

Hebros—Chief river in Thrace. It is frequently mentioned in the worship of Dionysos. 105, 429

Hekabe (Hekuba)—The wife of Priam and mother of Hektor. 461

Hekate—Earth goddess associated with sorcery, magic and ghosts, and worshiped by night at crossroads. 159

Hekatonymos—Proper name. 543

Hektor—Son of Priam and husband of Andromache, Hektor was the hero of the defense of Troy. He was killed by Achilles in Homer's *Iliad*. 187

Helen—Daughter of Zeus and Leda, a goddess of extraordinary beauty. As wife of Menelaos, she was seduced and taken to Troy by Paris and so became the overt cause of the Trojan War. 106, 124, 230, In. Stesichoros, 288, 290, 426

Helikon—Mountain in Boiotia named after a legendary man. 410, 474

Heliodora—Girlfriend of Meleagros. 491, 492, 496

Heliodora—Proper name. 538

Helios—God of the sun. 281, 293, 431

Hellas/Hellenes—The Greeks called their country Hellas and themselves Hellenes. 2, 107, In. Hipponax, Te. Pindaros, 425, 446

Hephaistion—A writer on prosody in the second century A.D. In. Glykon

Hephaistos—God of fire and metalwork. 12, 195, 281

Hera—Sister and wife of Zeus; the goddess of marriage. 33, 76, 149, 174

Herakleitos—Proper name. 468

Herakles—Son of Zeus and Alkmena (whose husband was Amphitryon). Herakles was a strongman and the performer of the Twelve Labors. In. Stesichoros, 293, 305, 378, 426, 429, 437, 571

Hermes—Herald of the gods. Patron of heralds, travelers and thieves. Also guide of the souls to the underworld. 178, 252, 312, Te. Hipparchos, 407, 408, 410, 411, 412, 465

Hermesianax—Greek elegiac poet of the fourth century B.C. In. Photius, Te. Mimnermos

Hermione—Daughter of Menelaos and Helen. Hermione's beauty, as a demigod, did not match the beauty of her mother, Helen. 230

Hermione—Birthplace of Lasos in the Argolid of the Peloponnesos. 309, Te. Mimnermos, In. Lasos, Te. Lasos

Hermobios—Proper name. Te. Mimnermos

Hermogenes—Proper name. 531, 532

Hermon—Proper name. 529

Hermos—A river of Asia Minor. 280

Hero—One of Sappho's friends. 194

Herodotos—The "Father of History," according to Cicero. Herodotos (fifth century B.C.) was the first author to make the events of the past the subject of research and verification. Te. Solon

Herondas—A writer of mimes and a native of Kos or Miletos (ca. 300-250 B.C.). In. Hipponax

Hesiod—Early Greek poet of the eighth century B.C., and author of *Works and Days* and the *Theogony*. Te. Phokylides, 356

Hesperides—Divine maidens, guardians of the golden apples in the garden of the gods. Islands in "distant" west. 281

Hesperos—The evening star, the son of Astraios or Kephalos or Atlas and Eos (Dawn) and father of the Hesperides. 138, 251, 441, 502

Hesychios—Greek grammarian of Alexandria whose chief literary work was a Greek lexicon. He lived in the fourth century A.D. Te. Lasos, Te. Simonides

Hieron—Tyrant of Syracuse and victor in the Olympic and Pythian games. In. Pindaros

Himera—A Greek city on the north coast of Sicily. Probably the birthplace of the poet Stesichoros. 421

Hipparchos—Brother of the Athenian despot Hippias. He was murdered in 514 B.C. In. Anakreon, In. Simonides, In. Lasos, 407, 408

Hippias—Son of the despot Peisistratos, Hippias was despot of Athens from 527 to 510 B.C. In. Anakreon, 387, In. Hipparchos, Te. Hipparchos

Hippokrateia—Mother of the poet Korinna and wife of Acheloodoros. Te. Korinna

Hippolytos—A Christian writer (fl. A.D. 200). Te. Hippon

Hipponax—Of Ephesos, a Greek iambic poet (fl. 546-520 B.C.). In. Hipponax, Te. Simonides, 312, 313

Hippon—A physical philosopher (fl. 430 B.C.). Te. Xenophanes

Homer—First epic poet of Greece. His poems were the basis of Greek literature and education. The author of the *Iliad* and the *Odyssey*. Te. Archilochos, In. Kallinos, In. Tyrtaios, 63, In. Alkman, Te. Alkaios, In. Sappho, In. Stesichoros, 314, 356, In. Bakchylides, 574

Horace—One of the main Roman lyric poets (65-8 B.C.). In. Archilochos, In. Alkaios, Te. Mimnermos, Te. Pindaros, Te. Bakchylides, In. Philodemos

Hymen—God of marriage. 177

Hyperboreans—A fabulous people living in a land of perpetual sunshine somewhere beyond the North Wind. Poets use "Hyperborean" to mean most northerly. 107, 426

Hyperion—A Titan, son of Uranus (Heaven) and Ge (Earth), and father of Helios (Sun), Selene (Moon) and Eos (Dawn). Sometimes refers to Helios himself. 293

Hypnos—God of sleep. 498

Ianthemis—Proper name. 72

Ibykos—Greek lyric poet of Rhegium, Ibykos lived at the court of Polykrates at Samos. In. Ibykos, In. Stesichoros, In. Anakreon

Ida—In Homer, Ida is the summit from which the gods watched the battle of Troy. 187

Ida—Zeus was said to have been brought up in a cave in Mt. Ida, in central Krete. 431

Idas—The kidnapper of Apollo's beloved Marpessa. 430

Idyl, Idyll—"A little picture," or a short poem depicting a pastoral scene. In Theokritos

Ilios—Son of Tros and founder of Ilium (Troy). 187

Ilium—Another name for Troy. 106, 149, 187, 461

Iole—Daughter of King Eurytos. Herakles sought to marry her. 429

Ion—Poet and playwright of fifth century B.C. Te. Pindaros

Ionia—A district on and off the west coast of Asia Minor, colonized by the Ionians. This is the region where early Greek literature and philosophy developed. 143, In. Stesichoros, In. Mimnermos, In. Anakreon, 431

Ionic—The Greek dialect of Ionia. In. Archilochos, In. Anakreon, In. Theokritos

Iphimenes—Proper name. 373

Iranna—Proper name. 240

Iris (Thaumantias)—The goddess of the rainbow and a messenger of the gods. She is the wife of Zephyros, the West Wind. 353

Iros—A beggar in the house of Odysseus. 606

Ismarian—Of Ismaros, a town in Thrace which produced excellent wine. Poets use the term "Ismarian" as equivalent to "Thracian." 26

Isokrates—Fourth of the "Ten Attic Orators," he was a great teacher of rhetoric. Te. Phokylides

Isthmos—The isthmus at Corinth separating the mainland from the Peloponnesos. 364, 421

Istrian—The Istrian land was by the Istros or Danube River. 426

Iulus (Ascanius)—Son of Aeneas. Te. Pindaros

Jason—Leader of the Argonauts who set sail in the *Argo* to find the Golden Fleece. 210, 278

Justinian—Roman emperor at Constantinople (A.D. 527-565). In. Paulus Silentiarius

Kadmos—Son of Agenor and founder of the Greek city of Thebes. Te. Pindaros

Kallia—Father of Megakles. 369

Kallimachos—Alexandrian grammarian and poet of the third century A.D. In. Kallimachos, In. Archilochos, In. Hipponax, In. Theokritos

Kallinos—Of Ephesos. The earliest Greek elegiac poet (fl. 700 B.C.?). In. Tyrtaios

Karia—A district of western Asia Minor. 580

Karystos—A town of Lakonia. 82

Kastalia—A nymph who, when pursued by Apollo, threw herself into a spring on Mount Parnassos. The spring was henceforward held sacred to Apollo and to the Muses. The latter were often called Kastalides. 107

Kastor—See Dioskouri. 75, 95

Kean—Of the island of KEOS. 431

Kenaian Zeus—Of the temple to Zeus in Kenaion. 429

Keos—An island of the Kyklades and birthplace of Simonides. In. Simonides, In. Bakchylides

Keres—Spirits of death. 282

Kerkidas—Greek poet of an uncertain date. Wrote in lyric meters on ethical subjects. In. Hipponax

Kerkylas—Husband of Sappho. In. Sappho

Kephissos—Chief river in the Athenian plain. 107

Kithairon—A mountain in Boiotia named after a legendary man. 375, 410

Klazomenai—City of Asia Minor. The birthplace of Anaxagoras. In. Hipponax

Kleësisera—Proper name. 72

Kleinorides—Proper name. 340

Kleïs—Name of Sappho's daughter, also her mother, and perhaps a friend. In. Sappho, 142, 231, 232

Kleomenes—King of Sparta, 520-489 B.C. Te. Telesilla

Klymenos—A god of the nether world. 390

Klytaimnestra—Wife and murderess of Agamemnon and mistress of Aigisthos. Murdered in turn by her son Orestes. 289

Knidos—City of Asia Minor and the home of the famous astronomer Eudoxos. 449

Knossos—An ancient town in Krete. "Knossian" is the equivalent of "Kretan." 148, 421, 431

Koios—Father of Leto, the mother of Apollo. 245

Kolophon—One of the twelve Ionian cities of Asia Minor and said to be the birthplace of Homer; the site of the oracle of Apollo Klarios. Te. Kallinos, In. Mimnermos, 283, In. Xenophanes, 346

Konon—Proper name. 548

Korax—Proper name. 506

Koressos—A hill. 512

Korinna—Greek lyric poetess (fl. ca. 500 B.C.). Believed to have been the instructor of Pindaros. In. Korinna, 409, 414

Kos—One of the islands called Sporades, home of Hippo-krates, and a favorite place for men of letters. Theokritos lived there at one time. Te. Kallinos, In. Theokritos, In. Meleagros

Kratinos—Athenian poet of the Old Comedy. Te. Hippon

Krete (Crete)—A large island in the Mediterranean where Minoan civilization flourished. 148, 183, 382, 431, 580

Krines—Father of Simonides. Te. Simonides

Kritias—Proper name. 317

Kriton—Rich citizen of Athens and friend of Sokrates. 528

Kroisos—The last king of Lydia. His wealth and power at-tracted the poet Solon to his court. Te. Solon

Kronian Pelops—Pelops was the great grandson of Kronos. 426

Kronos—Father of Zeus. 119, 410, 431

Kyklades—A group of islands in the Aigaian Sea lying in a circle around the sacred island of Delos. In. Bakchylides

Kyllene—The highest mountain in the Peloponnesos, sacred to Hermes, who had a temple on the summit. Hermes is some-times called "Kyllenios." 312

Kynoskephalai—"Dog Heads," two hills in Thessaly where Flaminius defeated Philip of Macedonia (197 B.C.). In. Pin-daros

Kyprian/Kypris/Kytherea—See APHRODITE. 150, 154, 203, 234, 235, 294, 297, 302, 478, 479, 483, 598

Kypros—An island in the Mediterranean and one of the chief seats of worship of the goddess Aphrodite. 86, 151, 156, 187, 259, Te. Solon.

Kyrene—A Greek city of North Africa between Carthage and Alexandria. In. Kallimachos, 467

Kyrnos—Friend of the poet Theognis; also the Greek name for Corsica. Poems which specifically mention Kyrnos by name are considered authentic poems of Theognis. In. Theognis, 392, 393, 394, 396, 405

Laïs—A famous courtesan of Corinth, known for her beauty. 446

Lakedaimonians—Spartans. In mythology Lakedaimon, a son of Zeus and Taygete, married Sparta and named his city after her. 359

Lakonia—A region of the Peloponnesos. Sparta was its capital. Te. Alkman, 82

Lampsakos—City of Asia Minor celebrated for its wine. The chief seat of worship for Priapos. 387

Lasos—A poet and teacher of Pindar. Te. Apollodoros

Leda—Mother of Helen and Klytaimnestra, Kastor and Polydeukes. Wooed by Zeus in the disguise of a swan. 95, 246, 426

Lelantine War—A war between Chalkis and Eretria for possession of the plain watered by the Lelantos (ca. 690 B.C.). 27

Leonidas—King of Sparta, 487-480 B.C., died heroically at Thermopylai, fighting against the invading Persians. 340, 362, 367

Leontichos—Proper name. 470

Lesbos—An island in the Aigaian Sea off the coast of Mysia in Asia Minor. Birthplace of the poets Terpandros, Sappho, and Alkaios. Te. Terpandros, In. Alkaios, 116, In. Sappho, Te. Sappho, 213, 231, 321, 453, 580

Lethaios—A small tributary of the Maiandros River in Asia Minor. 318

Leto—Mother of Apollo and Artemis. Leto was worshiped in connection with her children. 65, 196, 426

Leukadian Rock—Promontory on the island of Leukas from which suspected criminals were cast into the sea. Birds were attached to them in order to break their fall. This rock gave rise to the story that lovers leapt from it to escape the pangs of love. See PHAON. In. Sappho

Lokria—Greek city in southern Italy, known for its laws. 423

Longinus—Greek philosopher, literary critic and grammarian of the third century A.D. Teacher of Zenobia. Te. Pindaros

Loukianos/Lucian—Greek writer of the second century A.D. In. Loukianos, Te. Simonides

Lydia—A district in Asia Minor between Mysia and Karia. An early seat of Asian civilization, exerting an important influence on the Greeks. 31, In. Alkman, Te. Alkman, 72, 112, 124, 141, 208, 231, 280, 309, 316, 346, 379

Lykambes—Nobleman, father of Neoboule, loved by Archilochos. In. Archilochos, 34, 52

Lykas—Proper name. 375

Lysippos—Famous Greek sculptor, contemporary of Alexander. Te. Praxilla

Lysis—Pythagorean philosopher and teacher of Epaminondas. Te. Lamprokles

Macedon/Macedonia—A region of northern Greece; birthplace of Alexander the Great. In. Malanippides, Te. Melanippides, In. Timotheos

Maia—Daughter of Atlas and Pleione. The eldest and most beautiful of the Pleiades. Mother of Hermes. 312

Manes—Proper name. 464

Marathon—Village in Attica and the site of the crucial battle between the Persians and the Athenians in 490 B.C. In. Simonides, 366

Mauros—Proper name. 552

Marpessa—Daughter of Evenos and wife of Idas. 430

Media—North of Persia, its inhabitants were the Medes. When Media was conquered by Persia, Mede and Media became synonymous in Greek for Persian and Persia. 457

Megakles—Proper name. 369

Megalostrata—Loved by Alkman. 78

Megara—Capital of Megaris, a district of Greece. One of the four divisions of Attica. In. Theognis, Te. Theognis

Megastrys—Lover of King Gyges. 309

Megatimos—Proper name. 46

Megistes—Proper name. 342

Megistias—An Akarnanian seer who at Thermopylai refused to return to the rear and died in battle. 368

Melanchros—Tyrant of Lesbos in 610 B.C. Overthrown by Pittakos. In. Alkaios

Melanippos—Friend of Alkaios. 119

Melanippos—Proper name. 467

Meles—Proper name. 286

Melissa—Nymph, discoverer of honey, and from whom bees received their name. Here used as a proper name. 511

Melos—An island in the Aigaian and the most westerly of the Sporades. In. Melanippides

Menandros—Proper name. 527

Menelaos—Son of Atreus and younger brother of Agamemnon. The rape of his wife, Helen, by Paris, caused the Trojan War. 290

Menippos—Cynic philosopher of Gadara in Syria (fl. 250 B.C.). Te. Meleagros, 501

Menippos—Proper name. 517

Meniskos—Father of Pelagon. 239

Messene—Country in Peloponnesos. Defeated three different times by Sparta in the Messenian Wars (seventh century B.C.).

Mika—Probably a shortened form of "Mnasidika," a rival who had gone over to the rival house of Penthilos, ruling nobles of Mytilene. 233

Miletos—A great city of Asia Minor. Birthplace of Anaximandros, Anaximenes and Thales. In. Phokylides, In. Timotheos, Te. Timotheos, 515

Mimnermos—Greek elegiac poet and contemporary of Solon. In. Mimnermos, Te. Kallinos, In. Phokylides

Mimnes—Proper name. 311

Minoa—City in Amorgos founded by Simonides. Te. Simonides

Minos—Son of Zeus and Europa, Minos was a mythical king of Krete, ruling at Knossos. Later he was one of the judges of the underworld. 431, 459

Mnasidika—A friend of Sappho's who appears to have deserted her. "Mika" is probably a shortened form of "Mnasidika." 215

Molione—The twins of Molione were the Aktoridai; they were killed by Herakles. 305

Molouris—A rock on the coast near Megara, from which Ino and Melikertes threw themselves into the sea. 373

Muses—Daughters of Zeus, the nine Muses lived on Mount Helikon where they presided over the arts and sciences. Te. Archilochos, 65, 66, Te. Alkman, 78, 91, Te. Sappho, 162, 163, 164, 255, 302, 314, 396, 410, Te. Pindaros, 423, 426, 452, 453, Te. Theokritos, Te. Leonidas, Te. Meleagros, 501, 586

Myiskos—Proper name. 489

Mykonians/Mykonos—Of Mykonos, an island in the Aigaian Sea. The place where Herakles defeated the giants. 6, 40

Myrsilos—Tyrant of Mytilene who probably caused the exile of Sappho and Alkaios. In. Alkaios, 118, 232

Myrtis—Teacher of Korinna. 413

Mysians—Of Mysia, a district in the northwest corner of Asia Minor. 333

Mytilene—Chief city of Lesbos. 112, 116, In. Alkaios, In. Sappho, 142, 219, 232

Nanno—A flute-girl to whom Mimnermos addressed his elegies. 72, In. Mimnermos, Te. Mimnermos

Naxos—An island in the Aigaian. 26, 46

Nearchos—Proper name. 545

Nebuchadnezzar—King of Babylon from 605 to 562 B.C., who captured Jerusalem. In. Alkaios

Neleian Pylos—Neleus of Pylos, son of Poseidon and king of Pylos in the western Peloponnesos. Brother of Pelias. 283

Nemea—Valley in Argolis where Herakles slew the Nemean lion, and where the Nemean games were held. 535

Nemesis—The Greek goddess of retribution for sinful excess; also of compensation for good fortune. 549

Neoboule—Daughter of Lykambes, loved by Archilochos. In. Archilochos, 34

Nereids—Sea nymphs. Fifty in number, they were the daughters of Nereus. 234

Nereus—The god of the sea. His empire is the Aigaian Sea. Sometimes he is called the Aigaian. 106, 205, 431

Nero—Emperor of Rome (A.D. 54-68). In. Lucillius, In. Leonidas

Nessos—A Centaur who tried to seduce Herakles' wife Deianeira. 429

Nikilla—Proper name. 525

Nikon—Proper name. 517

Nikoteles—Proper name. 466

Niobe—Daughter of Tantalos, wife of Amphion. Niobe once boasted that her family was larger than Leto's. To avenge this insult Leto killed twelve of Niobe's children. Niobe is a stock figure of bereavement. 196

Nymphs—Female divinities of a lower rank represented as beautiful girls living in the mountains, forests, meadows and waters. 421, 455

Oichalia—City of Euboia. 429

Oineos—Father of Perimede. Te. Asios

Oinos—Town of Lakonia. 82

Olympia/Olympians—A plain in Elis where the Olympian Games were held. This plain was sacred to Zeus. 13, 261, 377, 421

Olympian Games—Athletic events celebrated at Olympia from earliest times in Greece every four years. 426, 534

Olympos—A range of mountains separating Thessaly and Macedon. The home of the gods. 320, 426

Onogla—A town in Lakonia. 82

Orestes—Son of Agamemnon and Klytaimnestra and avenger of his father's murder by Klytaimnestra and Aigisthos. In. Stesichoros

Orthria (Orthia). A goddess. Later Artemis Orthia. 72

Ortygia—An island near Syracuse, claimed as birthplace of Artemis. Ortygia was also a name associated with Artemis, and hence another name for Delos, where Artemis, according to most accounts, was born. 307

Ossa—A mountain in the north of Thessaly associated with the war of the giants. 375

Ovid—Roman poet (fl. ca. 23 B.C.). In. Sappho

Palatine Anthology (Greek Anthology)—Collection of Greek epigrams started by Constantine Cephalas and finished by

Planudes. Te. Hipponax, Te. Platon, Te. Kallimachos, In. Kallikteros, In. Ammonides, In. Diophones

Pan—Goat-footed god of shepherds and flocks. 455, 472, 473

Pandion—Father of Prokne, who became a swallow, and Philomela, who became a nightingale. Reputed grandfather of Theseus. 197, 431

Paphian—Of Paphos, and therefore of Aphrodite. Aphrodite was born in the foam near the city of Paphos in Kypros. 84, 174, 446

Parrhasios—Painter and poet, second century B.C. In. Parrhasios, 437

Parmenides—Philosopher of Elea and founder of the Eleatic school of philosophy. Born ca. 510 B.C. Te. Phokylides, Te. Theognis

Parnassos—A mountain in central Greece thought to be the dwelling place of Apollo and the Muses. Also sacred to Dionysos. 107

Paros—An island in the Aigaian Sea. Birthplace of Archilochos. In. Archilochos. Te. Archilochos, 4

Parthians—Of Parthia, a country of Asia. The Parthians were a warlike people and their savagery became proverbial. 571

Pasiphile—Proper name meaning literally "lover of everybody." 16

Paulus Silentiarius (Paul the Silentiary)—An officer of the Justinian household (fl. A.D. 540) and a Greek poet of epigrams. In. Silentiarius, In. Agathias Scholastikos

Pausanias—Greek travel writer of the second century A.D. Author of *Hellados Periegetes*, a guide to the cities and monuments of Greece. Te. Asios, Te. Telesilla, Te. Timotheos

Peisistratos—Despot of Athens, 561-527 B.C., with intervals of exile. In. Simonides, In. Hipparchos

Peitho—Personification of persuasion, the goddess of seductive charm. 160, 188, 302

Pelagon—A fisherman. 239

Peleus—King of the Myrmidons at Phthia in Thessaly. The father of Achilles and the husband of the nereid Thetis. 106

Pelias—Son of Poseidon and Tyro. Ordered Jason to search for the Golden Fleece and was later butchered by his own daughters, and boiled. 538

Pelion—A mountain of Thessaly. 375

Peloponnesos—The southernmost part of Greece, connected with the central region by the Isthmus of Corinth. In. Lasos, In. Bakchylides, Te. Bakchylides, In. Anyte

Glossary and Index

Polykrates—Tyrant of Samos in the second half of the sixth
century B.C. He maintained a sumptuous court at Samos
where Anakreon and Ibykos lived. In. Ibykos, In. Anakreon
Polypas—Proper name. 397
Polyphemos—A Cyclops and son of Poseidon. 503
Porphyrio—Neoplatonic philosopher (fl. A.D. 270). Te. Bak-
chylides
Poseidon—The brother of Zeus and the lord of the sea and of
earthquakes and horses. 53, 335, 430, 431
Praxagoras—Father of Theokritos. Te. Theokritos
Praxinoa—Friend of Sappho. 142
Praxiteles—A famous Greek sculptor of the fourth century B.C.
444
Priam—King of Troy at the time of the Trojan War and hus-
band of Hekuba. The father of fifty sons and daughters,
including Paris. 106, 187
Priapos—God of fertility and of the herds. Son of Aphrodite
and Dionysos, he is represented as a grotesque character
with a phallic symbol. It was customary to inscribe short
poems on his statues. 471, 472, 476
Priene—A city of Ionia near Mount Mykale. 19
Proklos—A teacher of the Neoplatonic school and an advocate
of paganism (A.D. 412-485).
Proklos—Proper name. 603
Propertius—Roman poet of the first century B.C., only rivaled
by Catullus as a love poet. In. Leonidas
Ptolemy II—King of Egypt in the second century B.C. Patron of
literature and science. The Holy Scriptures were translated
into Greek by his command. In. Theokritos
Pygelia—A city in Ionia near Ephesos. 316
Pyrrha—A town of Lesbos. In. Alkaios
Pythagoras—Celebrated Greek philosopher and mathemati-
cian. 349, Te. Lamprokles, Te. Platon
Pythia/Pythian Healer—A surname for Apollo. 429, 474, Te.
Pindaros
Pytho—Older name for Delphi, where the Pythian priestess
gave her ambiguous answers and where Pythian games
were held. The Apollo of Delphi was the Pythian Apollo.
421
Pythokleides—A Pythagorian musician of the sixth century
B.C. Te. Lamprokles
Python—Proper name. 337

Quintilian—Roman rhetorician. His greatest achievement was
a complete system of rhetoric. Te. Archilochos, Te. Alkaios, Te. Simonides, Te. Pindaros, Te. Parrhasios

Rhegium—A Greek town on the coast of Bruttium in the south of Italy. This was the cross-over point for Sicily. In. Ibykos, Te. Ibykos, Te. Hippon, 438

Rheia (Rhea)—Greek earth goddess, daughter of Ge and Uranus, wife of Kronos and mother of Demeter, Hestia, Zeus, Hera, Hades, Poseidon. 410

Rhipé—A legendary mountain range in northern Greece. 74

Rhodes—The most easterly of the islands of the Aigaian. In. Timokreon, Te. Timokreon, 580

Rhodo—Proper name. 558, 569

Rome—Capital of modern and ancient Italy. In. Mimnermos

Salamis—An island off the coast of Attica, where the Greeks defeated the Persian fleet of Xerxes in 480 B.C. In. Solon, Te. Solon, 267

Salmydessos—A town in Thrace on the coast of Euxine. The name originally referred to the whole coast. 3

Samos—An Ionian island off the southwest coast of Asia Minor. Birthplace of Pythagoras. In. Asios, Te. Asios, In. Ibykos, In. Simonides, Te. Simonides, In. Anakreon, In. Hippon

Samosata—Capital of the province of Commagene, north of Syria. Birthplace of Loukianos. In. Loukianos

Sappho—Lyric poet of Eresos or Mytilene in Lesbos. In. Sappho, In. Terpandros, 109, 142, 143, 147, 152, 166, 169, 201, 245, 259, In. Ibykos, Te. Bakchylides, In. Theokritos, In. Anakreon, Te. Anakreon

Sardis—Ancient city of Asia Minor, capital of Lydia. In. Alkman, 77, 122, 141, In. Anakreon, 577

Scholiast—Refers to an ancient commentator whose scholia, marginal commentaries of a Greek text, have been preserved. Te. Lamprokles, Te. Bakchylides, Te. Hippon

Semele—Mother of Dionysos. 98

Semiramis—Assyrian queen known for her beauty, reputed founder of Babylon. 563

Seneca (Lucius Annaeus)—Roman philosopher and playwright born in the first century B.C. Convicted in a conspiracy to assassinate Nero, Seneca was ordered to commit suicide. Te. Anakreon

Seven Against Thebes—Polyneikes and six other warriors in a force against Eteokles in Thebes. In. Korinna

Sicily—A large island separated from Italy by the Straits of Messina. Birthplace of Stesichoros and Theokritos, it was one of the principal points of contact between Roman and Hellenistic cultures. 1, In. Sappho, In. Stesichoros, In.

Simonides, Te. Theognis, 402, In. Pindaros, 426, In. Bakchylides, In. Bion, Te. Bion

Sigeion—Promontory near Troy, commanding the mouth of
the Hellespont. In. Alkaios

Simonides—Greek elegiac poet of the seventh century B.C. The
uncle of Bakchylides, he is famous for his heroic epigrams.
In. Simonides, 65, In. Stesichoros, In. Lasos, Te. Hipparchos, In. Timokreon, Te. Bakchylides

Sirens—Fabulous creatures of the sea that drove men to de-
struction by their song. Often represented as birds with
the heads and torsos of women. 72

Sirios—The Dog Star in the constellation of the Great Dog.
23, 72, 97, 304

Siris—A river in southern Italy. 1

Sisyphos—A mortal who persuaded Hades to release him from
Hell for a time. When he failed to return, he was forcibly
retrieved by Hermes. He was punished by being forced to
roll a stone up a hill, only to find it ever rolling back
again into the valley. 119

Skamandronymos—Father of Sappho. In. Sappho

Skapte Hyle—A town of Thrace. Te. Bakchylides

Skopelinos—Flute teacher of Pindar. Te. Lasos

Skylla—A fearful monster with twelve feet and six heads.
Once the lover of Poseidon, Skylla was turned into a monster by her rival Amphitrite. 490

Skythia—Region of southern Russia. 72, 373

Smyrna—City on the Ionian coast. 56, In. Mimnermos, 283, 309

Smyrneid—A long poem on the history of Smyrna. In. Mimnermos

Sokrates—The most famous of Greek philosophers. Left no
writings and is chiefly known through the works of Plato
and Xenophon. In. Parrhasios, Te. Melanippides, Te. Stesichoros, 445, 448, In. Platon

Solon—Athenian poet and statesman (ca. 640-559 B.C.). He was
one of the "Seven Wise Men." In. Solon, 267, In. Phokylides

Sophokles—Athenian tragic poet of the fifth century B.C. Te.
Pindaros

Sparta—The capital of Lakonia and the most important city of
the Peloponnesos in historical times. In. Tyrtaios, In. Alkman, Te. Tyrtaios, 57, In. Terpandros, Te. Terpandros, 66,
104, 303, 362, 365, 367, 368, 402, Te. Telesilla, 430, Te.
Timotheos

Spercheios—A river in the southern part of Thessaly, named
after the river god Spercheios. 368

Sporades—A group of scattered islands in the Aigaian Sea, off

Telephos—Father of Philetas. Te. Kallinos

Telesikles—Father of Archilochos. In. Archilochos

Teos—An Ionian city on the coast of Asia Minor. The birth-place of Anakreon. In. Anakreon, 573

Tereus—The son of Ares and King of the Thracians. Husband of the sisters Prokne and Philomela. He deprived Philomela of her tongue. 578

Thasos—A rocky island off the coast of Thrace. In. Archilochos, 1, 2

Thebe—A city of Mysia, in the northwest of Asia Minor. 187

Thebes—Principal city of Boiotia. Birthplace of Pindar and Korinna. Te. Korinna, Te. Pindaros, 58, 582

Themistokles—A celebrated Athenian statesman and archon in 493 B.C. Important for his role in the second Persian War. In. Simonides

Theognis—Elegiac poet (fl. second half of sixth century B.C.). He is the best preserved of the Greek elegists. In. Theognis, In. Alkaios, Te. Phokylides

Thermopylai—A narrow pass between the spurs of Mount Oita and the sea, the gate of eastern Greece, where the Spartans delayed the Persians in a famous battle in 486 B.C. In. Simonides, 361, 365, 368

Theron—Tyrant of Akragas, victor in the Olympian games. See title of Olympia III. In. Pindaros, 426

Theseus—Attic hero who went to Krete to slay the Minotaur. In. Bakchylides he is represented as a son of Poseidon. 431

Thessaly—The largest division of Greece. The mythological home of the Centaurs and also a country of magicians. 77, In. Anakreon, In. Simonides, 375

Thetis—A Nereid, daughter of Nereus and Doris. The mother of Achilles. 106

Thrace—The northern part of the Greek peninsula. 3, 29, 297, In. Anakreon, 322, 351

Thucydides—Greek historian who started a history of the Peloponnesian War. Te. Bakchylides

Thylakis—Proper name. 72

Thyone—Mother of Dionysos, Semele, was raised to the sky, deified as a star, and known as Thyone. 149

Timas—One of Sappho's companions. 155, 243

Timokritos—Celebrated Greek lyric poet of Rhodes (fl. fifth century B.C.). 336

Titans—Monstrous children of the primeval couple of Uranus and Ge. 345

Tithonos—Lover of Eos (Dawn) who left him each morning. Through the prayers of Eos he became immortal but he did not retain his youth and so became synonymous with decrepitude. 236

Troizen—District in the Peloponnesos; southeast of Argolis, where Theseus was born. 431

Trojan War—A war between the Achaians and the people of Troy in the first quarter of the twelfth century B.C.; the subject of Homer's *Iliad*. Te. Simonides, In. Stesichoros

Troy/Trojan—Ancient city near the Skamandros River on the Asian shore of the Hellespont. 122, 124, 288, 582, In. Alkaios

Tyndareos/Tyndareus—King of Sparta and husband of Leda. 294

Tyros (Tyre)—A famous city of the ancient world on the coast of Phoenicia. In. Meleagros, Te. Meleagros, 489, 501

Tyrrhenians—The Tyrrhenians (Etruscans) were defeated by Hiero in a great sea battle off Naples in 474 B.C. 370

Tyrtaios—Athenian elegiac poet of the seventh century B.C. In. Tyrtaios, In. Kallinos

Vergil—Roman poet of the first century B.C. Author of the *Aeneid*, the story of the founding of the Roman Empire. In. Philodemos, In. Theokritos, In. Leonidas

Xanthippe—Wife of Sokrates and said to have been a shrew. 443

Xanthippos—Father of Perikles. In. Anakreon

Xanthos—A river of Troy. 72

Xenophon—Historian, author of the *Anabasis*; lived in the fifth century B.C. Te. Bakchylides, Te. Parrhasios, Te. Melanippides

Zenobios—Rhetorician of the second century A.D. Te. Praxilla

Zenonis—Proper name. 527

Zenophila—Girl friend of Meleagros. 494, 498

Zephyr/Zephyros—The West Wind. 428

Zeus—The ruler of the gods, wielder of the thunderbolt and seducer of many goddesses and women. 13, 49, 56, 59, 64, 91, 95, 96, 98, 107, 112, 147, 149, 161, 245, 282, 293, 318, 374, 376, 418, 421, 449, 482, 516, 518, 535, 603

Zozime—Proper name. 565

Bibliography

✧✧

TEXTS IN GREEK

Adrados, Francisco R. *Líricos griegos: elegiacos y yambógraphos arcaicos*, 2 vols. Barcelona, 1956. (Includes translation and notes in Spanish.)

Bowra, C. M. *Pindari carmina*. Oxford, 1935.

Diehl, Ernst, and others. *Anthologia Lyrica Graeca*. 3d ed. Leipzig, 1949-. (Three fascicles out of six thus far issued.)

Gow, A. S. F. *Bucolici Graeci*. Oxford, 1952.

Heitsch, Ernst. *Die griechischen Dichterfragmente der Römischen Kaiserzeit*. Göttingen, 1961.

Lobel, Edgar, and Denys Page. *Poetarum Lesbiorum Fragmenta*. Oxford, 1955.

Moore, J. A. *Selections from the Greek Elegiac, Iambic, and Lyric Poets*. Cambridge, Mass., 1947. (English commentary.)

Murray, Gilbert, and others. *The Oxford Book of Greek Verse*. Oxford, 1930.

Page, Denys. *Poetae Melici Graeci*. Oxford, 1962.

Powell, John U. *Collectanea Alexandrina*. Oxford, 1925.

Smyth, Herbert Weir. *Greek Melic Poets*. London and New York, 1900. Repr. 1963. (English commentary.)

Snell, B. *Bacchylidis carmina cum fragmentis*. Leipzig, 1949.

TEXTS IN GREEK WITH ENGLISH TRANSLATION

Barnstone, Willis. *Sappho: Lyrics in the Original Greek with Translations by Willis Barnstone*. New York, 1965.

Edmonds, J. M. *Elegy and Iambus; Anacreontea*. 2 vols. London and New York, 1931.

———. *The Greek Bucolic Poets*. Rev. ed. London and New York, 1928.

———. *Lyra Graeca*. 3 vols. 2d ed. London and New York, 1928.

Farnell, L. R. *The Works of Pindar*. 3 vols. London, 1930-32. (English commentary.)

Gow, A. S. F. *Theocritus*. 2 vols. Cambridge, England, 1952. (English commentary.)

Jebb, R. C. *Bacchylides: The Poems and Fragments*. Cambridge, England, 1905. (English commentary.)

Mackail, J. W. *Select Epigrams from the Greek Anthology*. 3d ed. London, 1911.

[293]

Page, Denys. *Sappho and Alcaeus.* Oxford, 1955. (English commentary.)
———. *Select Papyri: Vol. III, Literary Papyri: Poetry.* Rev. ed. London and Cambridge, Mass., 1942.
Paton, W. R. *The Greek Anthology.* 5 vols. London and New York, 1916-18.

TRANSLATIONS WITHOUT GREEK TEXT

Barnard, Mary. *Sappho.* Berkeley and Los Angeles, 1958.
Fagles, Robert. *Bacchylides: Complete Poems.* New Haven, 1961.
Fitts, Dudley. *Poems from the Greek Anthology.* New York, 1938.
Higham, T. F., and C. M. Bowra. *The Oxford Book of Greek Verse in Translation.* Oxford, 1938.
Lattimore, Richmond. *Greek Lyrics.* 2d ed. Chicago, 1960.
———. *The Odes of Pindar.* Chicago, 1947.
Mills, Barriss. *The Idylls of Theokritos.* West Lafayette, Ind., 1963.

STUDIES

Bowra, C. M. *Early Greek Elegists.* Cambridge, Mass., 1938.
———. *Greek Lyric Poetry.* 2d ed. Oxford, 1961.
Burn, A. R. *The Lyric Age of Greece.* London, 1960.
Fränkel, Hermann. *Dichtung und Philosophie des frühen Griechentums.* 2d ed. Munich, 1962.
Körte, Alfred. *Hellenistic Poetry,* trans. Hammer and Hadas. New York, 1929.
Mackail, J. W. *Lectures on Greek Poetry.* London and New York, 1926.
Norwood, Gilbert. *Pindar.* Berkeley and Los Angeles, 1945.
Symonds, John Addington. *Studies of the Greek Poets.* New York and London, n.d.
Webster, T. B. L. *Greek Art and Literature, 700-530 B.C.* New York, 1960.

REFERENCES

Oxford Classical Dictionary.
Pauly-Wissowa, *Real-Encyclopädie der classischen Altertumswissenschaft.*
Rose, H. J. *A Handbook of Greek Literature.* 4th ed. London, 1951.
Schmid-Stählin, *Geschichte der griechischen Literatur.* Munich, 1920-48.

Concordance

BARNSTONE	EDMONDS	DIEHL
Archilochos		
1	21, 21A	18
2	52	54
3	97A	79
4	51	53
5	53	55
6	54	56
7	4	5a
8	23	21
9	43	43
10	11	12
11	9, 13	7
12	12	10
13	74	74
14	160	
15	29	25
16	17	15
17	72	72
18	47	34
19	97	102
20	184	1 (adespota)
21	142	
22	56	58
23	61	63
24	118	103
25	1	
26	2	
27	3	
28	103	112
29	6	6
30	58	60
31	25	22
32	14	13
33	19	17
34	71	71
35	84, 85	104, 118
36	68	69
37	35	37
38	114	51, 117
39	48A	50
40	78	78
41	8	9
42	65	66

Concordance

Barnstone	Edmonds	Diehl
43	97B	80
44	22, 13	20, 10
45	66	67a
46	18	16
47	33	32
48	31	27
49	88	94
50	27	30
51	30	26
52	94, 143	88
53	10	11
54	63	64

Kallinos

55	1	1
56	2	2

Tyrtaios

57	10	6, 7
58	14	11

Semonides

59	1	1
60	3	3
61	2	2
62	6	6
63	*Sim.* 97	29

Terpandros

			Page
64	1	1	698
65	3	*Carm. Pop.* 49	941
66	6		

Alkman

67	70, 25	93, 92	40, 39
68	36	58	89
69	47	37	56
70	56	54	93
71	49		
72	1	1	1
73	28	15	82
74	64	59	90
75	2B	2	2
76	16	24	60
77	2A	13	16
78	130	101, 102	59
79	46	49	17
80	138	55	19

[296]

Concordance

Barnstone	Edmonds	Diehl	Page
81	137	56	20
82	139	53	92
83	61	105	91
84	142	110	102
85	89	72	79
86	24	35	55
87	131	36	58
88	39, 17, 19, 20	64, 65, 62, 19	54, 170, 53, 35
89	26	94	26
90	67	109	125
91	50	40	28
92	164		176
93	13	7	14c

			Lobel and Page
Alkaios			
94	166	98	Z44
95	14	78	B2
96	157, 158	90, 91	Z14, 11
97	161	94	Z23
98	163	96	Z22
99	156	70	C1
100	159	92	Z39
101	133	50	Z27
102	85	103	Z36
103	141	135	Z21
104	81, 92, 175	101	Z37
105	17	77	B13
106	120	74	B10
107	1	1	Z1
108	18	142	Z41
109	86, 92, 175	67, 123, 139	A10B
110	19	54	Z34
111	28, 29		
112	69	42	D11
113	77A	117	F5
114	160	87	Z24
115	37, 38	30, 118, 119, 120	Z2, A6
116	76	27	D16
117	50	31	H2
118	70	43	D12
119	122	73	B6
Sappho			
120	80	103	118
121	1a		
122		Suppl. pp. 39, 70	98a
123	74	108	120
124	38	27a	16

Concordance

Barnstone	Edmonds	Diehl	Lobel and Page
125	111	94	
126	27	19	38
127	54	50	47
128	2	2	(Page II)
129	53	47	52
130	139	118	143
131	78	113	145
132	12	11	160
133	3	4	34
134	19	15	123
135	94	Alc. 94	Alc. 347b
136	16	13	42
137	138	121	136
138	32	133	104b
139	133	156	
140	69	56	54
141	86	98	96
142	82	95	92
143	83	96	94
144	81	137	131
145	48	40, 41	49
146	43	34a	24a
147	1	1	(Page I)
148	(Bowra, p. 196)	5, 6	2
149	40	28	(Page VI)
150	135	114	102
151	134	156	
152	75	110	159
153	31		198
154	103	107	140
155	87	99	101
156	123	87	134
157	7, 8	8	40
158	9	9	33
159	24	145	i.a. 23
160	33		200
161	68	57	53
162	101	90	128
163	129	154	127
164	10	10	32
165	128	134	126
166	126	144b	133 (16A)
167	55	143	144
168	150, 151	116, 117	105 a, c
169	30		125
171	161	127	115
172	(Bowra, p. 221)	39	30
173	65	54	43
174	147		

Concordance

Barnstone	Edmonds	Diehl	Lobel and Page
175	163	130	113
176	155, 156, 158	128	112, 116
177	148 (11. 2-7)	123	111
178	146	135, 136	141
179	160, 16a	129, 128	117, 112, 116
180	154	124	110
181	52	46	51
182	84a		197
183	112, 114	88, 93	154, i.a. 16
184	157		
185	164	131	114
186	159	53	107
187	66	55 a, b	44
188	(Lobel, p. 80)	98	96
189	89	48	48
190	121	150	155
191	125	144a	133 (16)
192	98	61	57
193	51	45	i.a. 5
194	73	62	i.a. 11
195	70	Alc. 9a	Alc. 349b
196	140	119	142
197	122	86	135
198	100	92	148
199	71	58	55
200	120	151	138
201	Alc. 124, Sa. 119	Alc. 63, Sa. 149	Alc. 384, Sa. 137
202	58	49	50
203	45	36	22, 9-19
204	23	20	36
205	41	31	20
206	72	60	56
207	110		204
208	20	17	39
209	105	85	100
210	21	142	152
211	56, 57	42	46
212	61, 60, 59, 62	138, 139	156, 167
213	148 (11. 9-11)	115	106
214	117	80	81b
215	115	63	82a
216	93	141	i.a. (1. 2)
217	137	126	158
218	50A (App.)	156B	139
219	(Robinson, 122)		196
220	142	51	i.a. 25
221	22	18	129 (1. 2)
222	29	147	163
223	18	14	37

Concordance

BARNSTONE	EDMONDS	DIEHL	LOBEL AND PAGE
224	107	111	122
225	96	140	i.a. 5 (1. 3)
226	13	37	26 (11. 2-4)
227	106	52	146
228	141, 141A	125, 106	149, 151
229	46	38	27
230	44	35	23
231	130	152	132
232		Suppl. pp. 39, 70	98b
233		70	71
234	36	25	(Page V)
235	37	26	15
236	118	65a	58
237	118B (App.)	67	63
238	118A (App.)	66	62
239	145	159	
240	116	64	91
241	113A, B		201 i.a. 18
243	114	158	
244	(Treu, p. 16)		Inc. 27
245	(Treu, p. 7)	102 (1. 1)	Alc. 304
246	97	105	166
247	99	100	121
248	28		172, 188
249	124	146	129 (1. 1)
250	14	12	41
251	149	120	104a
252	85	97	95
253	42	32	21
254	108	109	150
255	11		193
256	76, 77	59	147
257	Lyra Graeca III, p. 438	Fr. Mel. Mon. Adesp. 18	
258	34	24	4
259	om.	68	65
260	177	16	157

Solon

261	36	24	
262	28a	4	
263	9	10	
264	32	23	
265	24	14	
266	15	4	
267	1	2	
268	21	22	

Concordance

BARNSTONE	EDMONDS	DIEHL
269	41	27
270	25	12
271	17	17
272	14	15
273	27	19

Mimnermos

274	1	1
275	3	3
276	(Greek Anthology IX 50)	
277	6	8
278	7	11
279	12	7
280	14	13
281	8	10
282	2	2
283	10	12

Phokylides

284	9	11
285	3	2

Asios

286	1	1

Stesichoros

287	87		256
288	18	11	192
289	43	15	219
290	15	10	187
291	2	2	179a
292	5	4	184
293	8	6	185
294	12	17	223
295	52, 53, 54	22, 23, 24	232, 244, 245
296	36, 37, 38	12, 13, 14	210, 212, 211

Ibykos

297	1	6	286
298	9	11	303b
299	2	7	287
300	4, 5	9, 10	317
301	7	13	315
302	6	8	288
303	65		339
304	3	12	314
305	34	2	285
306	28	23	313
307	23	21	321

Concordance

Barnstone	Knox	Diehl
Hipponax		
308	78	70
309	54	3
310	1	12
311	68	45
312	57, 59, 60	24a, b, 25
313	61	20
314	89	77
315	67	42
316		(Andrados 92)
317	69	67

Barnstone	Edmonds	Diehl	Lobel and Page
Anakreon			
318	1	1	348
319	47	34	398
320	25	52, 53	378, 379
321	15	5	358
322	84	88	417
323	75	27	396
324	48, 49	45, 46	413, 414
325	21	17	376
326	104	79	428
327	122		446
328	138		439
329	97	54	388
330	4	4	360
331	116		
332	9	11	363
333	36	20	377
334	101	87	424
335	6	6	362
336	150		
337	158		
338	89	92	443
339	149		
340	162		
341	29	60	437
342	68	65	416
343	69	44	395
344	56	37	410
Xenophanes			
345	1	1	
346	3	3	
347	23	19	
348	34	30	
349	6a	6	
350	18	16	
351	14, 15, 16	12, 13, 14	

Concordance

Barnstone	Edmonds	Diehl	Lobel and Page
352	30	26	
353	32	28	
354	27	23	
355	29	25	
356	11	10	
357	28	24	

Simonides

358	129	122	
359	126	121	
360	133	116	
361	21	5	531
362	116	87	
363	65	37	579
364	124	95	
365	119	92	
366	117	88	
367	122	120	
368	120	83	
369	141	84	
370	136	97	
371	128	119	
372	95	53	
373	142	80	
374	27	13	543
375	159	142	
376	37	20	508
377	181	148	
378	39	23	509
379	152	140	
380	144	129	
381	60	28	571
382	156	138	
383	70	56	604
384	22	6	521
385	73	45	586
386	26	7	523
387	139	85	
388	98		648
389	32, 33	10, 11	526, 527

Lasos

390	1	1	702

Line numbers standard in all editions

Theognis

391	1069-1070
392	183-192
393	181-182
394	173-178

[303]

Concordance

Concordance

BARNSTONE	EDMONDS	DIEHL	PAGE
Bakchylides			
427	7		
428	75		
429	11		
430	15		
431	12		
Praxilla			
432	1	2	747
433	5	3	754
434	2	1	748
435	4		750
Parrhasios			
436	2	2	
437	3	3	
Hippon			
438	1	1	
Melanippides			
439	1	1	757
Timotheos			
440	15	11	800
Platon (Plato)			
441	2	5	
442	1	4	
443	8	3	
444	7	2	
445	6	1	
446	11	15	
447	4	7	
448	5	8	
449	17	24	
450	(Greek Anthology IX 51)	30	
451	14	28	
452	12	17	
453	16	16	
454	(Greek Anthology XVI 13)	27	
455	(Greek Anthology IX 823)	26	
456	18	14	
457	13	10	
458	9	9	

[305]

Concordance

BARNSTONE	EDMONDS	DIEHL
459	(Greek Anthology VII 268)	29
460	14	28
461	3	6

GREEK ANTHOLOGY

Diphilos

462	XI 439

Anyte

463	IX 313
464	VII 538
465	IX 314

Kallimachos

466	VII 453
467	VII 517
468	VII 80
469	VII 318
470	VII 277

Theokritos

471	IX 437
472	IX 338
473	VI 177
474	VI 336
475	(Idyll 7, 11, 135–146)

Leonidas of Tarentum

476	X 1
477	XVI 230

Asklepiades

478	V 169
479	V 85
480	V 210
481	V 162
482	V 64

Mnasalkas

483	IX 333

Theodoridas

484	VII 282

Poem numbers standard

Moschos

485	IV

Concordance

Concordance

BARNSTONE	GREEK ANTHOLOGY

Parmenion

516	V 34

Nikarchos

517	XI 406
518	XI 113
519	XI 241
520	XI 252
521	XI 242
522	XI 186
523	V 38

Lucilius

524	XI 310
525	XI 68
526	XI 192
527	XI 139
528	XI 165
529	XI 264
530	XI 240
531	XI 257
532	XI 190
533	XI 80
534	XI 75
535	XI 258
536	XI 277
537	XI 105
538	XI 256
539	XI 93
540	XI 215
541	XI 133
542	XI 391

Leonidas of Alexandria

543	IX 348

Traianus

544	XI 418

Ammianus

545	XI 226

Loukianos (Lucian)

546	XI 430

Dionysius Sophistes

547	V 81

Concordance

[309]

Concordance